PRIVACY IN THE MODERN AGE

PRIVACY IN THE MODERN AGE

The Search for Solutions

Edited by
**Marc Rotenberg,
Julia Horwitz, and Jeramie Scott**

THE NEW PRESS

NEW YORK
LONDON

This publication has been made possible, in part, with a grant from the MacArthur Foundation. The views expressed are those of the authors, and do not necessarily represent the views of their employers, the MacArthur Foundation, or EPIC.

Published in the United States by The New Press, New York, 2015
Distributed by Perseus Distribution

ISBN 978-1-62097-107-9 (hc.)
ISBN 978-1-62097-108-6 (e-book)
CIP data is available

The New Press publishes books that promote and enrich public discussion and understanding of the issues vital to our democracy and to a more equitable world. These books are made possible by the enthusiasm of our readers; the support of a committed group of donors, large and small; the collaboration of our many partners in the independent media and the not-for-profit sector; booksellers, who often hand-sell New Press books; librarians; and above all by our authors.

www.thenewpress.com

Composition by dix!
This book was set in Minion

Printed in the United States of America

2   4   6   8   10   9   7   5   3   1

CONTENTS

FOREWORD

Few issues today are more widely debated than the impact of technology on privacy. Edward Snowden has kept news organizations busy since his decision to reveal the surveillance capabilities of the National Security Agency. The NSA has gathered up the telephone records of every American, as well as the personal communications of foreign leaders and the Internet browsing records of their citizens. So extraordinary is the data-gathering capability of the NSA that the agency has budgeted millions of dollars just for air-conditioning to keep cool its giant supercomputers.

But it is not only a spy agency that inspires headlines. Target lost the credit card records of 40 million American consumers in a data security breach. Home Depot beat that record and lost 56 million records. Advertising software tracks users across the Internet. Detailed medical records are available for sale. Students are subject to endless testing that generates data subject to endless review. Travelers to the United States are fingerprinted. Small robots patrol schoolyards. And we have still ahead data breaches that involve biometric identifiers, surveillance systems that massively identify people in a crowd, and firms that have leapt from the Internet to track people in physical space and record activities in their homes.

There is a temptation when confronted with these stories to utter some version of "Privacy is dead. Get over it." Popular variants include, "You have no reasonable expectation of privacy," "What did you expect? You posted it on the Internet," and "Hey, it's free. If you don't like it, you don't have to use it."

The contributors to this anthology adopted a different strategy. They put fatalism aside and instead of simply describing problems, they set out solutions; they took seriously the dictum of Thomas Edison: "What man creates with his hand, he should control with his head." It's a new approach to the privacy debate, one that assumes privacy is worth protecting and that there are meaningful policy responses to pursue.

We begin the collection by tracing our own efforts to create an organization, the Electronic Privacy Information Center or "EPIC," specifically tasked with focusing public attention on emerging privacy and civil liberties issues. Over our first twenty years, we have had some successes and some setbacks. Our recent anniversary provided an opportunity to assess what is working and what more needs to be done.

Open government advocate Steven Aftergood takes on the classic paradox of privacy in his contribution—the critical role of transparency in ensuring accountability. Aftergood notes, "Transparency alone cannot dictate or imply what the outcome of a particular privacy or national security debate ought to be. But disclosure of the basic facts of government operations is what makes it possible for the debate to take place." In openness, there is greater protection for privacy.

Computer scientist Ross Anderson views the U.S. debate

from across the Atlantic and asks what the U.S. legacy will be when others look back at the technologically dominant superpower in the early part of the twenty-first century. It is not just a matter of legacy. "How the U.S. treats foreigners now will not just set the tone for our generation, but will shape how the world works and the way people are treated in future generations—once U.S. supremacy has passed the way of the British empire, the Spanish empire, and the Roman empire."

Christine L. Borgman and her coauthors, experts in information policy and educational institutions, took on the practical challenge of developing a privacy framework for the largest university system in the United States. As they explain, "Today's research universities face a plethora of competing challenges in the privacy arena." The outcome is a remarkable blend of privacy principles, institutional structures, formal responsibilities, and public accountability.

Ryan Calo, a leading researcher in the field of robotics, thinks it is already time to pass laws and to create an agency to monitor our mechanized friends. As he writes, "Society should look to this issue now, as we stand knee-deep in waters that will only rise."

Danielle Citron, a law professor who explores issues of gender, combines several threads of privacy culture when she points to growing concerns about "revenge porn." Her proposal is clear. "The law needs updating again to combat destructive invasions of sexual privacy facilitated by networked technologies."

Leading privacy campaigner Simon Davies focuses on recent developments in Europe, where the Snowden revelations have given way to massive calls to update privacy laws and limit data flows to America. Davies suggests that even a fractured Europe is likely to unite in this effort.

A. Michael Froomkin, one of the forefathers of cyberlaw, considers the policy nuts and bolts of identity management. At its core, the challenge is to allow individuals to disclose to others only that which is required in a technological environment where almost everything is transferred by default. The solution is subtle but profound. "In its most robust form, we would have true untraceable pseudonymity powered by payer-anonymous digital cash."

Deborah Hurley, writer, lecturer, and policy adviser, traces the development of modern human rights instruments concerning privacy and notes the leadership role of the United States, beginning with the Universal Declaration of Human Rights in 1948. But she also finds that in recent years, the United States has lost its way and urges it to adopt comprehensive federal legislation to protect personal data and privacy.

From a European perspective, Kristina Irion looks at the safeguards and accountability of mass surveillance in Europe and the United States and how these affect transatlantic relations. Irion points "to asymmetries between countries that are precisely at the core of the transatlantic rift over mass surveillance."

Jeff Jonas, a designer of analytic software systems with privacy safeguards, takes as a given that "surveillance society is inevitable and irreversible" as well as "irresistible." So, what is to be done? Jonas proposes several techniques—transfer accountability, attribute anonymization, data expiration, and audit trails—that could help reduce privacy risks.

Harry Lewis, an educator, computer scientist, and university administrator, makes the case for anonymous speech, but also cautions, "Among the responsibilities of civic life is to speak in our own voices when we can, and to take anonymous words seriously only if their anonymity is understandable."

Anna Lysyanskaya, also a tech expert, makes the case for cryptography. In theory, the opportunities are boundless. In direct terms, Lysyanskaya explains that cryptography gives us "tools for getting the best of both worlds: accountability for wrongdoers and yet privacy for everyone else."

Gary T. Marx, a pioneer in the field of technology and privacy, restates his challenges to the various techno-fallacies that often characterize contemporary discourse. He wisely concludes that "subjecting surveillance and privacy-hungry technologies to critical analysis . . . hardly guarantees a just and accountable society, but it is surely a necessary condition for one."

Aleecia M. McDonald, a researcher and policy analyst, takes a close look at several of the current techniques for privacy protection, including DuckDuckGo, PGP, and Tor, and uncovers increasing interest in privacy-enhancing technologies after the Snowden disclosures.

Dr. Pablo G. Molina, an educational administrator and ethicist, looks squarely at the challenges academic institutions face. "Three major actors are responsible for these data leaks and organizational abuses: academic administrators, educational entrepreneurs, and hackers." His solution is equally straightforward: "To ensure the privacy of educational information, we must influence the behavior of these three agents. We need better laws, better technologies, and better advocacy."

Peter G. Neumann, a security researcher, describes the current state of network security as "abysmal." Systems are riddled with vulnerabilities. They are inherently untrustworthy and fail by accident and by attack. Neumann recommends a "holistic approach that encompasses dramatic technological improvements, procedural efforts that are more than palliative best practices, legislation, . . . enforcement, and common sense. As usual," he writes, "there are no easy answers."

Helen Nissenbaum, a computer scientist and professor of media, culture, and communications, helped reframe the modern debate when she proposed that privacy was about "contextual integrity." The concept received the backing of President Obama with the release of the Consumer Privacy Bill of Rights in 2012. In this essay, Nissenbaum revisits the claim, clarifying its purpose and arguing for an interpretation that places the interests of the individual above the design of technology.

Frank Pasquale, a law professor who studies corporate culture, points to deeper questions about the interplay between academic study and business research. Drawing on the Facebook emotional manipulation study, Pasquale warns that the "corporate 'science' of manipulation is a far cry from academic science's ethics of openness and reproducibility."

Dr. Deborah Peel, MD, the founder of Patient Privacy Rights, points with increasing urgency to the loss of individual control over medical record information. The reasons are many: the transition from paper to the digital world, the emergence of complex payment systems, and the collapse of barriers between health care providers and marketing firms. The solution, Peel believes, can emerge when the health care industry will "be as accountable and transparent with our health data as banks are with our money."

Can free expression be preserved in the online world? Stephanie E. Perrin, an advocate for NGOs, speaks directly to the Internet

Corporation for Assigned Names and Numbers (ICANN), the organization that governs the Internet, when she proposes, "The ability to have an anonymous domain registration would benefit those who exercise their rights of free speech in dangerous territories, or who are fleeing abuse and persecution."

Noted copyright scholar Pamela Samuelson asked whether copyright might come to the rescue of privacy. Considering a recent series of decisions from federal courts, she notes a new strategy emerging, though also cautions about the possible impact on First Amendment interests.

Bruce Schneier has long been interested in the quality of the public debate about the future of privacy. What motivates us to act? What leaves us feeling powerless? He warns that "fear trumps privacy, because fear happens in a more primal part of our brain. And convenience trumps privacy, because convenience is real and immediate, while the harms from lack of privacy are more abstract and long-term." But he also remains hopeful about reasoned debate. "We need to think about these issues now and decide what sort of society we want to live in, rather than letting these changes just happen to us without consideration."

And Christopher Wolf, a leading attorney in the privacy field, provides an optimistic essay about how various privacy tools could help safeguard privacy even in our era of big data. Wolf concludes, "The prospects are good that thoughtful and concerned people will develop needed solutions with greater attention being paid to preserving privacy in our modern society."

Our final chapter is devoted to the Madrid Privacy Declaration, a seminal articulation of privacy rights, emerging challenges, and possible solutions. Adopted in 2009, the Declaration warns that "privacy law and privacy institutions have failed to take full account of new surveillance practices." The experts and NGOs who authored this statement point to well-known international frameworks and new strategies to safeguard the fundamental right of privacy.

Taken as a whole, these essays and the declaration describe a range of new challenges and also, maybe, forthcoming calamities. If Mr. Snowden and Target kept news organizations busy over the last few years, no doubt many of our authors are identifying the problems that we will read about in the years ahead. For this reason alone, these essays deserve a close read.

But if we continue to value the right to privacy, once described by Louis Brandeis as "the most comprehensive of all rights and the right most valued by a free people," then we must get about the hard work of finding solutions. In this respect, the contributors to this volume have made a double contribution: an insight into a new problem coupled with possible answers.

The contributors to this volume share another common attribute. They are also associated with the Electronic Privacy Information Center. Together with the other advisory board members and the EPIC staff, they have pursued the common purpose of working to safeguard privacy in the modern age.

We are grateful to the MacArthur Foundation for its support of this publication and related public policy work, and to the many other foundations and individuals who have helped make EPIC's work possible during the past twenty years. With this publication, we begin to chart our work program for the next twenty years. Privacy in the modern age is necessarily a search for solutions.

—Marc Rotenberg

EPIC: THE FIRST TWENTY YEARS
Marc Rotenberg

A little more than twenty years ago, the National Security Agency proposed a technical standard that would enable the routine surveillance of all communications in the United States. The "Clipper chip," as it was called, was an attempt to undermine the essential characteristics of robust encryption—the assurance of security and confidentiality. The key escrow standard, backed by the White House and pushed out to U.S. allies overseas, emerged just as the Internet was about to become the communications platform for much of the world.

At the time, a small group of lawyers with a commitment to civil liberties was working for the Computer Professionals for Social Responsibility in Washington, DC. We were working closely with technical experts, academics, and innovators. We were pursuing open government requests about emerging surveillance practices. We were testifying in Congress about legislative approaches to privacy protection. We were developing policy frameworks for the Internet. We were building coalitions with organizations in Washington, DC. And we ran a mailing list (and then a website) with a Mac SE and a 9,600-baud modem.

The Clipper chip proposal galvanized our community. Several of our advisers had helped create the technical standard to secure the Internet. Others were developing new approaches to privacy protection, such as techniques for "authentication without identification" that relied on the security of these underlying protocols. Others had strong philosophical beliefs about the freedom to innovate without the interference of government. Some had specific concerns that building in techniques for mass surveillance would create an Orwellian future. Of course, there was also disagreement. There was a genuine concern that in some circumstances new techniques for privacy could be exploited and cause great harm. An important debate was under way, among leading experts, about the future of the Internet and the protection of privacy. From this period, the Electronic Privacy Information Center, or simply EPIC, emerged.

Once it became clear that those most knowledgeable about the impact of the NSA proposal were strongly opposed, we built a national campaign on the Internet to stop the proposal. Over several months, we wrote letters, testified in Congress, and organized conferences. We organized the first Internet petition. More than fifty thousand Internet users supported a letter signed by forty-two experts in law, technology, and human rights, a large number in those days. In the spring of 1994 the White House announced it would drop the plan. We had, for the moment, a victory.

From the Clipper campaign, we moved quickly to establish a new type of organization. Our mission was clear: "to focus public attention on emerging privacy and civil liberties issues" and to protect privacy, the First Amendment, and Constitutional values. We would bring together technical experts and legal experts. We would also pursue advocacy in new ways. We would take advantage of the Internet, an emerging communications platform, although we were aware of the privacy risks. Our aim was not to avoid technology; it was instead to engage technology and shape it in ways that would respect fundamental rights. And we would measure our work by the results we achieved.

EPIC began as a project of the Fund for Constitutional Government, a private foundation established in 1974 to focus attention on government abuse. The match was good for us. The post-Watergate years were also the period when Congress passed the Privacy Act, strengthened the Freedom of Information Act, and held the Church Committee hearings. Later EPIC would incorporate as an independent nonprofit corporation. Throughout our many years, FCG remained by our side as a loyal supporter of our work.

We believed at the beginning that privacy was nonpartisan, a value widely shared by people across the country, and that there was no reason to draw political lines. In our consideration of the Clipper proposal, the party affiliations of our experts did not matter, and they would not matter going forward. John Anderson, the former independent presidential candidate and well-regarded constitutional defender, became our first chair and for many years a great advocate for the work of EPIC.

When we started EPIC, we made clear our desire to work closely with leading technical experts and legal scholars. We believed that this intersection was crucial to understanding emerging privacy issues. We also believed that outcomes were important. Experts are often brought together for the purposes of issuing a report or making recommendations. Our aim for the Clipper campaign was simply to stop the program, not to study it. And our strategy, at least at that time, succeeded.

We also looked closely at polling data to understand the

public perception of privacy, to assess trends, and to shape our priorities. It was significant that EPIC was established not long after a poll by the Lou Harris organization found 80 percent of Americans were concerned about threats to their privacy. More than two-thirds believed they had lost all control over personal information. Yet remarkably, 70 percent believed that privacy is a fundamental right comparable to "life, liberty and the pursuit of happiness." It was clear that most Americans wanted new protections in law to safeguard privacy.

Over the next twenty years, EPIC's program and activities would expand significantly. We developed a widely regarded Freedom of Information Act litigation program. We wrote amicus briefs on emerging privacy and civil liberties issues. We organized major conferences with policy leaders, technical experts, advocates, and academics. We testified often in Congress, and later before the European Parliament. We worked closely with other organizations. We helped shape key policy frameworks on privacy, encryption, computer security, open government, and the future of the Internet.

But it was the Clipper campaign that shaped the organization at the outset.

Here follows a brief summary of several of the key areas of EPIC program activities over our first twenty years.

THE CONSTRUCTION OF PRIVACY

Many pages have been filled attempting to define the right to privacy, to weigh it against competing rights, or to say what it is not. We decided at the outset not to go down those roads. At the time EPIC was established, the modern right of privacy, i.e., the articulation of privacy in the digital age, was well established. It was simply the rights and responsibilities associated with the collection of personal information, commonly described as "Fair Information Practices." This was the view set out by Willis Ware and his committee for the federal government in 1973. It was also the view reflected in the U.S. Privacy Act of 1974 and many laws in the United States, Europe, and elsewhere that followed. It is the view that we have spent more than twenty years promoting.

The Fair Information Practices provided the central conceptual framework for privacy rights in the digital age. Policies could be evaluated based on their adherence to FIPs; a strong commitment to FIPs meant strong commitment to the rights of individuals. Although there was some effort to dilute the essential framework by appending "Principles" or substituting "notice and choice" for the full panoply of rights and responsibilities, it is notable that twenty years after EPIC's founding, Fair Information Practices provide the starting point for much of the privacy policy in the United States and could be found most recently in the White House report on big data and the future of privacy. (Also worth noting is the conclusion from the president's science advisers that the "notice and choice" construction does not protect privacy, a point EPIC has argued for more than a dozen years.)

The right to anonymity flowed from the conception of privacy as a fundamental human right. Anonymity is the right to control the disclosure of one's actual identity, the bedrock of privacy. In the 1990s and before, EPIC followed closely challenges to identification requirements brought to the U.S. Supreme Court and noted with satisfaction that the Court would routinely uphold the claim of anonymity as well grounded in the First Amendment and the tradition of the Federalist Papers. Those with unpopular views, those who might be considered treasonous, needed privacy to protect their freedom of expression. We participated in both legal and technical campaigns to protect the disclosure of actual identity.

Our early work on caller ID, the first instance when the routine disclosure of actual identity arose in the design of the modern communication network, contributed significantly to our understanding of these issues. We recognized that in the relation between two people there was often a service provider in the background who could exploit the competing claims of disclosure and nondisclosure. We argued that individuals must retain the ability to control the disclosure of personal identity in the commercial realm similar to the right as against government in the constitutional realm. Much of our early work on identity preceded the emergence of social network services and the greatly amplified demands for disclosure of personal information.

Putting the pieces of FIPs and anonymity together, EPIC proposed that there should be new privacy-enhancing techniques that would "minimize or eliminate the collection of personally identifiable information." The goal was to encourage innovative solutions that would avoid the burdens associated with the obligations of Fair Information Practices while putting in place the technical measures that would enable communications. Several members of the EPIC advisory board, notably David Chaum, Whitfield Diffie, Peter G. Neumann, and Ron Rivest, helped us understand the role that technology could play in enabling new services with higher levels of privacy protection.

THE DEFENSE OF OPEN GOVERNMENT

Throughout EPIC's history, litigation under the Federal Freedom of Information Act has been one of our top program activities. We have pursued FOIA cases to uncover government programs that pose a threat to privacy and civil liberties. Dozens of the cases pursued by EPIC over the years have been reported in the national media, on everything from the original Clipper plan (internal agency memos found the program would weaken network security) to the Department of Homeland Security's monitoring of social media services (this led to a hearing in Congress) and the FBI's Next Generation Identification system (EPIC found that agency would permit a 15 percent error rate).

Our FOIA work has also received critical attention from the White House. Apparently, EPIC is one of several organizations whose FOIA requests are subject to "political review." This means that EPIC's FOIA work is of such consequence that the White House is notified when we make a request and is notified again prior to the release of documents. The practice may be unlawful, but we appreciate the recognition.

Throughout our twenty years, EPIC has expanded our FOIA practice in several dimensions. We continue to pursue FOIA requests to uncover government surveillance plans. We regularly post the documents we have obtained on our website and annually post a "gallery" of significant documents obtained under the Freedom of Information Act. We also now comment on agency FOIA practices to help ensure that the purposes of the act are fulfilled in practice. We have testified in Congress in support of proposals to strengthen open government. Working with other open government organizations, EPIC has also written several amicus briefs in support of open government claims. Most recently, we supported the efforts of the ACLU and the *New York Times* to obtain the memos describing the legal authority for the use of drones.

In the last few years, we have started a new course with the Georgetown University Law Center to train the next generation of FOIA lawyers. The class combines formal instruction with the actual mechanics of pursuing a FOIA request. This course grew out of our summer clerkship program and our long-standing commitment to helping young lawyers learn about open government.

We have also pursued open government matters to make a larger point about the relationship between the protection of privacy and the need for transparency. Simply stated, in modern democracies privacy and transparency are complementary goals that strengthen the rights of individuals and help hold government accountable. That was the understanding of the Congress that passed the Privacy Act of 1974 and strengthened the Freedom of Information Act the same year. It is also a view that can be attributed to Justice Louis Brandeis, who is known in the privacy world for his famous article on the right to privacy and his dissent in the *Olmstead* case, but also in the First Amendment world for helping to shape the robust modern First Amendment doctrine and for stating that "sunlight is often the best disinfectant." And it is the understanding of privacy and transparency agencies around the world that simultaneously defend both legal rights.

Properly conceived, a privacy organization will defend transparency.

THE EPIC AMICUS

Justice Brandeis is well-known among appellate lawyers for the creation of a style of amicus brief, a brief intended to advise a court, that emphasizes scientific evidence as apart from legal argument. Around the time that EPIC undertook the campaign against Clipper, we worked on a case with the Supreme Court advocate Paul Wolfson on the emerging problem of identity theft and the problems that might arise from the widespread dissemination of the Social Security number. He encouraged us to file an amicus brief to explain the risks of the SSN to the federal appeals court. Our brief contributed to a successful outcome in the case.

From that point forward we looked for opportunities to identify significant cases in which EPIC could play a role as a friend of the court. As a small organization, we knew we could produce only a small number of briefs each year. Almost as much time was devoted to reviewing dockets for significant amicus opportunities as was devoted to drafting the briefs. By the time we chose to file in a case, we had to be sure that we were pursuing the right case for the right reason. And once we identified a case, we would do everything possible to achieve a successful outcome. We reviewed as much of the relevant technical literature as we could acquire. We would look at government reports and the recommendations of expert groups from the National Academy of Sciences and elsewhere. Then we would turn to our expert advisers, who would revise, correct, and reframe our arguments.

Twenty years later, EPIC has filed more than fifty amicus briefs in federal and state courts, and approximately half of those with the U.S. Supreme Court. The cases cover many of the most pressing privacy and civil liberties issues of our time, from the collection of DNA and the search of cell phones to the interpretation of privacy statutes and right of information privacy. These briefs are often cited in the opinions of courts, or their echoes can be heard in the questions at oral argument or the reasoning of a panel.

Consistent with our mission, we seek to identify emerging privacy and civil liberties issues and to bring these points to courts when the issues are considered. The EPIC advisory board, with its unique mix of technical and legal expertise, has carried forward the best traditions of the Brandeis brief.

THE ROLE OF THE FTC

One of the first challenges we considered after establishing EPIC was how to strengthen privacy protections in the United States. The Privacy Act of 1974, the main privacy law in the United States, set out an omnibus approach for privacy protection in the public sector but left open the question of how best to regulate the collection and use of personal information in the private sector. A patchwork of law was emerging in the United States in the early 1990s that seemed inefficient and incoherent. Some personal information received protection; other information did not. Legal standards varied across sectors. There was no baseline expectation that personal information was entitled to legal protection.

At the about the same time, the integration of the European countries was moving forward and the need to harmonize national data protection laws was central to the European efforts. It was widely understood in Europe, although not so well understood in the United States, that establishing the Data Protection Directive was an effort to facilitate the free flow of information. Data transfers would simply not be safe unless adequate legal and technical protections were put in place first. (Twenty years later it seems the United States is now learning the value of the European insight.)

Legislative proposals were under consideration in Congress in the late 1990s, and until the events of 9/11 it seemed likely that the United States would adopt a general privacy law for commercial activity. In the meanwhile, new threats to privacy were emerging. The mailing-list industry was selling detailed personal information on American consumers, including children, without their knowledge or consent. There was no law to limit the practice and no agency charged with privacy protection. Congress could hold oversight hearings and draw public attention to a problem, but without a law in place, there was no mechanism for enforcement.

EPIC turned to the Federal Trade Commission. We wanted to adapt the agency's authority to investigate and stop unfair and deceptive trade practices to protect consumer privacy. But there was no precedent and no history for an FTC role in the privacy world. At first we would write letters, identifying problems and proposing an investigation. But the letters lacked the legal arguments and factual materials that would be necessary to persuade lawyers and agency commissioners. We also knew that any action by the agency would be discretionary. A clear foundation would be needed for the FTC to protect consumer privacy.

Over time, EPIC developed a new strategy for the FTC: we

would draft detailed complaints, modeled after the agency's own complaints, that would set out clearly the identities of the parties, the specific practices to which we objected, the legal authority for the agency's action, and the relief that the agency should establish. We filled these complaints with as much factual, authoritative information as we could find. Oftentimes, we would also include in an EPIC complaint to the FTC the opinions of experts or the concerns of consumers, expressed in their own words, as described in a blog or a user comment.

From the time we first wrote to the FTC in 1995 about the need to protect consumer privacy, EPIC has worked with a coalition of consumer and privacy organizations to establish many of the most significant decisions at the Federal Trade Commission that safeguard the privacy interests of consumers.

These include the early cases against ChoicePoint for selling sensitive information to a criminal ring engaged in identity theft (which produced the largest settlement in the FTC's history at the time) and Microsoft's Passport sign-on service, which raised concerns in the technical and security community (Microsoft would later develop a useful model for user-centric authentication, one of the early examples of how government action can lead to better technical solutions). They included also the matters involving Facebook (for changing the privacy settings of users) and Google (for opting users into Google Buzz).

More recently, the Federal Trade Commission took action against Snapchat for faulty business practices after EPIC filed a detailed complaint describing how the company misrepresented certain privacy features and failed to account for security weaknesses. The FTC acknowledged EPIC's concerns about

Facebook's acquisition of the messaging service WhatsApp in a recent letter to both companies, stating that it would open an investigation if Facebook were to change the privacy policies of WhatsApp.

In some respects the outcomes were better than we anticipated. The Federal Trade Commission would often take the core of an EPIC complaint and then find other practices we had missed. The remedies proposed were typically more sweeping than we had recommended. Once a consent order was in place, the agency would maintain oversight of the company's practices for twenty years.

In other respects the outcomes have been disappointing. Although the FTC announces far-reaching settlements, the commission is often reluctant to enforce its own orders. Substantial changes in business practices impacting user privacy would take place, but the Commission would remain silent. Just as the FTC expects companies to stand behind their privacy commitments, we expect the FTC to stand behind its legal orders. But that is not always the result.

COMPARATIVE APPROACHES TO PRIVACY PROTECTION

At about the time that EPIC was established, we became increasingly aware of the growing debate over privacy protection in other countries and how these differing approaches might impact practices in the United States. David Flaherty had recently published a landmark study comparing privacy protection in several countries. The emergence of the EU Data Protection Directive had focused the legal debate on the key question of the "adequacy" of national regimes. And scholars such as Colin Bennett asked a fundamental question about whether the tendency among policy frameworks would be toward divergence or convergence.

We were also in contact with Simon Davies, who had established Privacy International in London after a successful campaign against a national identity card in Australia. Under Simon's direction, Privacy International emerged as a leading force on the global privacy front and began to explore comparative approaches to privacy protection.

David Banisar, one of the cofounders of EPIC, imagined that we might be able to prepare a substantial international privacy survey, similar to the surveys conducted by Amnesty International and Human Rights Watch, by taking excerpts from the annual report of the U.S. State Department and extracting the sections concerning privacy in the individual country reports. The first survey was a couple dozen pages with a staple in the corner. Working with Simon Davies and others at Privacy International, legal experts, and NGO advocates around the world, our brief survey expanded. By 2006, the report was a 1,200-page compendium with almost 6,000 footnotes. It was presented at the annual meeting of the International Conference of Data Protection and Privacy Commissioners.

Over the years, the network of advocates grew, the reporting became more detailed, and the methodology became more comprehensive. We were interested in both the formal legal structures that countries established and the way that privacy was protected (or not) in practice. In a genre that tends to emphasize threats to privacy, we made a point of highlighting the successful campaigns of NGOs. It was oftentimes remarkable to read the details of those individuals and organizations who stood up for privacy, such as the teachers in South Korea who blocked the establishment of a student database or the protesters in Berlin who objected to RFID-enabled identity documents.

To this day, the EPIC report *Privacy and Human Rights: An International Survey of Privacy Law and Development*, prepared with the help and assistance of Privacy International and hundreds of experts, advocates, and scholars, is the most comprehensive report on privacy ever published. One of our shortcomings is that we have not been able to continue this project.

THE PUBLIC VOICE

EPIC is built on collaboration between technical experts and legal scholars. We also believe in the vital role that civil society plays in the protection of privacy and the future of the Internet. From the beginning EPIC has worked closely with NGOs to strengthen the voice of civil society. This practice emerged from the early efforts of Deborah Hurley, who recognized a need for civil society organizations to be at the table along with the business groups and government officials who were shaping technology policy at international organizations.

We started the Public Voice project in 1996 specifically to promote civil society participation in decisions concerning the future of the Internet. Working in collaboration with several international organizations, including the Organisation for Economic Co-operation and Development (OECD), we helped plan events for civil society organizations around the globe on a wide range of issues from electronic commerce and Internet governance to privacy protection and encryption policy.

Our aim was always to promote a constructive dialogue that would enable the formulation and adoption of policy frameworks that would address emerging issues while safeguarding fundamental rights. We recognized also the importance of innovation and economic growth. Our frequent collaboration with the OECD made it possible to develop policy frameworks that aligned the goals of modern economies with consumer protection.

The Public Voice project continued to be a strong presence at the annual International Conference of Data Protection and Privacy Commissioners, often cohosting events for NGOs and technical experts, in collaboration with Privacy International and others. At the OECD, the Public Voice provided the foundation for the establishment of the Civil Society Information Society Advisory Council (CSISAC), the "voice of civil society."

In addition to important institutional developments, the Public Voice also worked to help articulate NGO frameworks. Examples of these include the charter of CSISAC, which set out a broad civil society agenda for Internet policy, and the Madrid Privacy Declaration, a key policy document that affirmed international frameworks for privacy protection, identified emerging challenges, and set out concrete recommendations for democratic governments.

The Public Voice also played a role in Internet governance and the development of ICANN. For a period of time, EPIC had a leadership role with the Public Interest Registry, the organization that manages the .ORG domain, and later with the civil society advisory committee for ICANN. But progress in the world of ICANN was hard to find. Most of the effort was directed toward holding off bad proposals, rather than moving forward good ones. And it is discouraging to note that much of the privacy debate at ICANN remains focused on the same issues from twenty years ago, such as WHOIS privacy, and not the need to move much more purposefully to strengthen the security and stability of the Internet.

EPIC'S INTERNET PRESENCE

Today EPIC maintains two of the most popular Internet sites in the world for a search on the term *privacy*—EPIC.org and Privacy.org—but neither is particularly flashy. We still send our biweekly newsletter in ASCII. We have avoided many of the techniques intended to drive up readership. Only a few photographs will be found on our website. There is no advertising.

What we have done over twenty years is to rigorously assemble significant documents concerning privacy and to write as objectively and fairly as we can about emerging privacy issues, recognizing that we often have strong views as to what the outcome should be. Thus the EPIC website puts a premium on maintaining the primary-source documents on all matters that we pursue.

There are also in the EPIC website two distinct voices—the objective statements and summaries found in our home page items and issue pages, and the advocacy reflected in our briefs and testimony. Wherever possible we have tried to include competing points of view. We are particularly proud of our work on the various court cases we have pursued—the Freedom of Information challenges and the amicus briefs. These Web pages typically include a comprehensive listing of all relevant documents, useful summaries, and related news stories. We make a point of including all opposing views.

It may seem odd to draw attention to such mundane facts. But much of the Internet today is driven by strong opinion, targeted advertising, and tricks to promote rankings. We have avoided all of that and still ended up with a very successful Web presence.

EPIC'S ROLE IN WASHINGTON

People are sometimes surprised to learn that EPIC is not a lobbying organization. We rarely sign statements to Congress on pending legislation. We do not campaign for candidates or align with political parties. There is no online form to "contact your congressman."

This decision is purposeful. We decided at the beginning to develop a different strategy, better suited for the issues we were addressing and the way we believed change could be made. We took literally our role as an educational organization. We believed that it would be possible through creative advocacy, litigation, and public engagement to shape the policy debate and produce meaningful results. Ultimately it was not a lobbying campaign that stopped Clipper in 1994. It was collaboration between technical experts and legal scholars, the engagement of the public, the use of the Internet as an organizing platform, the pursuit of relevant documents under the FOIA, and a sustained presence in a national debate about the future of privacy.

These are the strategies that we developed and pursued during the first twenty years of the Electronic Privacy Information Center. We explore now how we might build on these strategies for the next twenty years.

PRIVACY AND THE IMPERATIVE OF OPEN GOVERNMENT

Steven Aftergood

Until recently, personal privacy might not have ranked very high on the list of reasons to favor open government; it would certainly have been eclipsed in prominence by arguments based on principles of democratic governance and government accountability. But following the unauthorized disclosure of highly classified intelligence programs to collect telephone metadata records in bulk, privacy concerns have emerged as among the most urgent and compelling drivers of secrecy reform.

Defenders of the classified bulk collection programs initially suggested that concerns about privacy were misplaced since "only metadata," not the actual contents of the communications, were being recorded. Some even argued that the deep secrecy of the bulk collection program somehow complemented and reinforced personal privacy. "You can't have your privacy violated if you don't know your privacy is violated," contended Representative Mike Rogers, the chair of the House Intelligence Committee, at an October 2013 hearing.

Steven Aftergood is a senior research analyst at the Federation of American Scientists.

But such efforts to justify the classified collection programs were quickly overwhelmed by a tide of bipartisan public criticism, and even erstwhile defenders of the status quo were soon endorsing or offering their own proposals for change. This turn of events raises important policy issues in many domains, but it has implications for the future of open government in particular.

SECRECY PRECLUDES PUBLIC CONSENT

While privacy is the nominal subject of the controversy, the core issue raised by classified bulk collection goes beyond the actual or potential infringement on privacy that it entails. Rather, the essential problem raised by secret bulk collection of telephone metadata records is the fact that the public was denied any opportunity to grant—or to withhold—its consent to this practice.

In this way, privacy concerns lead inexorably to the imperative of openness in government. The broad policy objective is not necessarily to defend personal privacy at all costs, but to ensure that national security policies that impinge on personal privacy are subject to public debate and approval. It is this dimension of public consent that was conspicuously absent in development and execution of the bulk collection program.

THE NEED TO INVIGORATE CONGRESSIONAL OVERSIGHT

One might have thought that Congress, in its regular exercise of checks and balances, would have represented public concerns about privacy and that it would have provided the requisite opportunity for consent. Remarkably, in this case, that did not happen.

In retrospect, it is clear that the congressional intelligence committees did not accurately gauge or reflect public attitudes toward bulk collection. For reasons that require further investigation, the congressional watchdog did not bark. To the contrary, the committees appear to have been enablers of the program. Even after the director of national intelligence publicly denied before the Senate Intelligence Committee that any sort of mass collection of records involving U.S. persons was taking place, members of the committee did nothing to correct the record, though they knew this assertion to be false.

It may be that the congressional oversight committees are simply less capable of performing a contemporaneous oversight function than might have been supposed or hoped for. (The Senate Intelligence Committee has only recently completed a report on CIA interrogation activities that took place a full decade earlier.) Even today, there is little sign that the intelligence oversight committees have been chastened by the public uproar over bulk collection, or that they have been moved to engage in any kind of critical reflection on their role in the controversy. But if Congress wished to become more sensitive to the actual range of public interests and concerns, that would go some distance to improving the quality and integrity of national intelligence policy, including privacy policy.

There are several initial steps toward this end that could be undertaken: The professional diversity of committee staff could be expanded to include more persons with expertise in privacy and civil liberties issues. The number of open public hearings, which have been sparse in the last several years, and the number of nongovernmental witnesses could be increased. The record of congressional intelligence oversight itself, which includes historically valuable classified materials dating back to the Church Committee of the 1970s, could be usefully declassified. Any progress in this direction depends on setting a new standard of expectations for congressional performance and responsiveness, which depends in turn on the efforts of advocacy organizations, and ultimately on the public will itself.

A NEW DAWN FOR TRANSPARENCY?

U.S. intelligence agencies had an unusual realization in the aftermath of the unauthorized disclosure of the bulk telephony metadata collection program: transparency is not necessarily a problem—it can serve their interests too. Declassification, the agencies discovered, can be used to correct errors in the record, can provide relevant context for public deliberation, and can help to counteract cynicism about official activities and motivations.

This realization has been translated into policy, up to a point, with tangible results: more classified government records about ongoing intelligence surveillance programs have recently been declassified than ever before. The number of pages of top secret records about bulk collection programs in particular that have been officially declassified is roughly double the number of pages leaked by Edward Snowden that have been published in the news media.

Several new government websites have been established to

publicize and disseminate declassified intelligence records, including records pertaining to the privacy interests of U.S. persons. For the first time ever, a presidential directive on signals intelligence was issued by President Obama in unclassified form. New policy debates have taken shape on previously remote topics such as the privacy rights due to foreigners abroad against clandestine surveillance, and the suspected role of U.S. intelligence agencies in weakening public encryption standards and stockpiling known vulnerabilities.

Significantly, the director of national intelligence, James R. Clapper, has affirmed the view that it would have been prudent and proper to seek public consent for the bulk collection of call records from the start. "Had we been transparent about this from the outset right after 9/11 . . . we wouldn't have had the problem we had," DNI Clapper told the *Daily Beast*. This belated official acknowledgment that greater transparency would have benefited the intelligence community all along creates a foundation for a new conversation about what is wrong with current classification practices and what can be done to rectify them.

INSTITUTIONALIZING OPENNESS THROUGH EXTERNAL REVIEW

Everyone, up to and including the president of the United States, recognizes that overclassification of information is a fact and a problem. While the problem can be diagnosed in different ways, most people will agree that the present system is biased in favor of classification. So the practical question is, what can be done to promote a more limited and more discriminating use of classification authority that yields less secrecy and that is more respectful of privacy?

One could imagine a revised executive order on national security classification that included a new prohibition against classifying in order to conceal infringements on privacy. But such formal limitations, like those prohibiting classifying to conceal violations of law or to prevent embarrassment, have not been notably effective. There is, however, another approach that may hold the key to significant, voluntary reductions in official secrecy.

That is to extend declassification authority beyond the circle of the original classifiers, and to subject agency classification decisions to external review and critique. In interesting ways, this is already being done. Between 1996 and 2012, an executive-branch body called the Interagency Security Classification Appeals Panel (ISCAP) completely overturned the classification judgments of executive-branch agencies in 27 percent of the cases that it reviewed, and it partially overturned classification decisions in another 41 percent of such cases.

This surprisingly productive record can be explained by considering the fact that the ISCAP, while fully committed to protecting legitimate national security interests, does not share all of the specific bureaucratic interests of the individual agencies whose classification judgments it rejected. Subjecting those individual agency classification decisions to an external evaluation (albeit still within the executive branch) has consistently yielded a reduction in secrecy. Having been validated in practice year after year, this basic principle could now be applied more systematically or to address particularized concerns.

So, for example, all U.S. intelligence classification guides—which are documents that present specific, itemized guidance on exactly what types of information are to be classified and at what level—could be delivered for independent review and critique to the Public Interest Declassification Board. The PIDB, created by statute, exists to, among other things, promote "the fullest possible public access to a thorough, accurate, and reliable documentary record of significant U.S. national security decisions and activities."

Agency classification guides could be designated for a more specifically privacy-related review by the Privacy and Civil Liberties Oversight Board. This board could be asked to identify current intelligence community classification practices that have significant implications for personal privacy, to assess their validity, and to recommend appropriate changes in secrecy policy. There are other isolated "best practices" for classification review that already exist and that could easily be incorporated throughout the intelligence community and the executive branch as a whole.

The Department of Energy has a formal regulation (10 CFR 1045.20) under which members of the public may propose declassification of information that is classified under the Atomic Energy Act. I have made use of this regulation myself. A similar provision could be envisioned by which the public could challenge the classification of privacy-related and other national security information throughout the government. While one can already request declassification review of a particular document, the proposed approach would go beyond that to challenge the classification status of an entire topical area.

The current executive order on national security information allows for classification challenges, but only by security-cleared employees who already have access to the information. Naturally, the key to a successful classification challenge is that it must be reviewed impartially by someone other than the original classifier. But that is entirely achievable. In fiscal year 2012, government employees filed 402 such challenges, one-third of which were granted in whole or in part.

To cite one more example of an existing best practice that could be widely replicated, the inspector general of the Environmental Protection Agency actively solicits public suggestions for audits and investigations that it could perform. This potentially places one of the most powerful investigative tools in government at the disposal of public-interest requesters (and not only of actual whistleblowers). Although only Congress has the power to legally compel an inspector general investigation, the EPA IG's receptiveness to a well-founded public "suggestion" could reasonably be expected to become standard practice.

In the end, of course, openness by itself does not change anything. Once the door to public participation has been opened, then anyone is free to enter.

WHAT GOES AROUND
COMES AROUND

Ross Anderson

Each nation gets its day in the sun, its chance to leave a mark. As a Brit, I'm proud of the fact that my nineteenth-century ancestors gave the world both technology (railways, steamships, electricity) and moral norms (universal education, the abolition of slavery, and of child labour, too). Now it's America's turn. America has already given us many great things, from the motor car to the Internet, and has maybe one more generation left in which to make a real difference.

The architecture of the Internet, and the moral norms embedded in it, will be a huge part of America's legacy. The network effects that dominate the information goods and services industries will give that architecture great longevity, just as the Roman standard cart axle of 4 feet 8½ inches is still our railway gauge today.

So what Americans inflict on foreigners now will massively influence what the world inflicts on all our descendants for generations to come. If America re-engineers the Internet so that the NSA can snoop more easily on people in Pakistan and

Professor Ross Anderson is Professor of Security Engineering at the Computer Laboratory.

Yemen and Iran today, then in 50 years time the Chinese will use it to snoop on Americans; in 100 years time perhaps the Indians will have the whip hand; and in 200 years it might be the United States of Africa.

There is also a curious disconnect here between the way the tech industry sees the world and the view from Washington. It's not just that almost everyone in DC considers Edward Snowden to be a traitor while almost everyone in the tech industry sees him as a whistleblower. The right coast and the left coast also have completely different views of the underlying economics, and don't even seem to realise that there's a gap.

The tech industry has many monopolies, because of three factors that become ever more important as everything goes online. First, network effects mean that the value of a network grows faster than the number of members, so its value to each member increases with its size. Second, there's technical lock-in; you can't use your iPhone apps if you move to Android. And third, while the capital costs of new products get ever higher, the marginal cost of providing for one more customer is lower—and often pretty well zero.

But while the left coast is acutely aware of increasing returns to scale, the right coast sees international relations as a zero-sum game in which one nation gains power as another loses it. And government folks' failure to understand network effects and geek ways of working leads to many unforced errors. The regulation of networked industries is poor, and public-sector IT projects are notorious: the Obamacare website was just the latest of many failures.

Yet, like it or not, technology is starting to change the business of government, including intelligence and defence. The

Snowden papers reveal that the NSA has been sharing intelligence with a growing network of nations worldwide; it's not just the traditional "Five eyes" partners of Canada, the UK, Australia and New Zealand, but Germany, Sweden, Israel, France and many others too. While India used to buy its jet planes from Russia during the Cold War, now it shares intelligence with the NSA. Why? Well, the NSA has the bigger network. As five eyes become fifteen, then 25, then 65, the intelligence world is becoming a shadowy clone of the United Nations, but minus Russia and China. (Or maybe it's Microsoft versus Apple all over again.)

There is also technical lock-in as a single market emerges for the firms who do wiretapping and surveillance equipment. In the old days, the Russian phone system was different, so the NSA needed different kit to tap it; but now everyone's using IP. This leads to some interesting moral dilemmas around exports. And in both defence and intelligence, capital costs go up as marginal costs go down. In the old days, you had to pay a man a salary to climb a telephone pole and attach a wiretap; now the marginal cost of wiretaps is zero (though the agencies spend billions on data centres, and leverage the further billions spent by the service firms, ISPs and telcos).

This system-of-systems is sustained by commercial surveillance—by watching what we do and showing us ads. But it enables the law enforcement and intelligence agencies of dozens of countries to watch us too. And the spread of devices with gesture interfaces, voice interfaces and touch interfaces will mean that pretty soon there will be cameras and microphones in pretty well every room of every house on earth.

So how will that be governed? The intelligence agencies mostly don't care about even their own citizens' privacy, let alone anybody else's. Snowden reveals that in a meeting about whether Five Eyes states had to minimise metadata revealing sensitive personal information about each others' citizens, only Canada insisted on minimisation. In other words, GCHQ was quite happy for the NSA to know whether a UK citizen like me had ever phoned a sexual health clinic—and the NSA was quite relaxed about GCHQ having the same information on Americans. In another case, the NSA was relaxed about its Australian counterpart wiretapping a US law firm that was representing the Government of Indonesia in a case where Australian interests were considered to be at stake. In other words, a foreign intelligence service violated a US law firm's attorney-client privilege, in the USA, using interception facilities largely provided by the US taxpayer. If that isn't a wake-up call, it's hard to know what might be.

So it's great that Obama's review panel suggested that the NSA start respecting the privacy of non-US citizens. But it doesn't go far enough. It's helpful too that the panel also suggests ending the bulk collection of metadata; while the government may be able to snoop on anybody, it should not be able to snoop on everybody. But it will be hard to design an Internet where the NSA can do bulk surveillance of foreigners but only targeted surveillance of Americans. If code is law, then architecture is policy.

Here is the core issue, the acid test of whether America really believes in universal rights. But it is a challenge to which America can rise, because of the way its concept of rights has expanded steadily over the generations. Once a nation has bought the idea that "All men are created equal", you eventually ask "blacks too"? It might take fourscore and seven years, but sooner or later the question can't be ducked any more. Then people ask "women too?" and so it goes: civil rights, gay rights, until eventually there's only one taboo left. The question now is "Foreigners too?"

NEW MODELS OF PRIVACY FOR THE UNIVERSITY

Christine L. Borgman (coauthored with
Kent Wada and James F. Davis)[1]

INTRODUCTION

Today's research universities face a plethora of competing challenges in the privacy arena. They aspire to provide welcoming spaces that encourage their communities to explore and to exchange new ideas. They must be good stewards of troves of highly sensitive data about their communities, such as student records and health information, and sensitive data collected by their communities, such as human subjects research data. Universities are uniquely concerned with academic freedom, because "the common good depends upon the free search for truth and its free exposition" ("Academic Freedom," 2014). Faculty and students alike must be able to conduct their research, within accepted guidelines, without exposing their data prematurely. These freedoms are balanced with the requirements of funding agencies and journals to release data that are subject to peer review and to open access policies, and of state open records laws for public universities. There is also a full

Christine L. Borgman, professor and presidential chair in information studies at UCLA, is the author of more than two hundred publications in information studies, computer science, and communication.

spectrum of data values that spans from public good, sharing, and collaboration to intellectual property and commercialization. Finally, privacy underpins an ethical and respectful environment for the entire university community.

The University of California, which is the largest public research university in the United States, with 10 campuses, 5 academic medical centers, and management of 3 national laboratories and more than 233,000 students and 190,000 faculty and staff, faces all of these privacy issues and more. In June of 2010, Mark Yudof, then president of the University of California, formed the Privacy and Information Security Steering Committee to perform a comprehensive review of the university's current privacy and information security policy framework and to make recommendations about how the university should address near-term policy issues and longer-term governance issues. The committee consisted of a broad cross-section of functional areas within the university and included representation from faculty, staff, and students. EPIC was among the groups consulted as part of the committee's research and deliberations. The final report, released January 2013, includes the UC Statement of Privacy Values and Privacy Principles, several recommendations, and an implementation timeline ("Privacy and Information Security Initiative, Final Report," 2014).

The report addresses the need to balance privacy with the many rights, values, and desires of our society and recognizes that technology, social norms, and policy evolve at differential rates. Ubiquitous access to, and creation of, information via mobile devices, social media paradigms, and virtual communities intersect with "real" life in unexpected ways, many of them privacy related. The framework offers a new, holistic approach to privacy and information security in universities. It provides a common vocabulary by distinguishing between types of privacy and explicating relationships between them and with security. It places privacy in the constellation of university values and legal, policy, and administrative obligations. It establishes principles and a governance model marrying academic and administrative interests that permits the institution to balance competing values and obligations for decision-making and policy development.

PRIVACY AND INFORMATION SECURITY

Privacy is about the individual. In the report, it is also about the agreement between the university and the individual that defines how the privacy of that individual is handled. Two types of privacy must be addressed in university values, principles, and policy:

- *Autonomy privacy:* an individual's ability to conduct activities without concern of or actual observation; it is related to concepts such as the First Amendment's freedom of association, anonymity, and the monitoring of behavior.
- *Information privacy:* the appropriate protection, use, and dissemination of information about individuals; it is about an individual's interest in controlling or significantly influencing the handling of information about him- or herself, whether it is an academic, medical, financial, or other record.

Information security, as distinct from privacy, supports the protection of information resources from unauthorized access that could compromise their confidentiality, integrity, and availability. Information resources include both infrastructure (such as computers and networks) and information (whether or not it is related to individuals). Information security supports, and is essential to, autonomy and information privacy.

The diagram below generally depicts the domains covered by autonomy privacy, information privacy, and information security, and the overlaps among them.

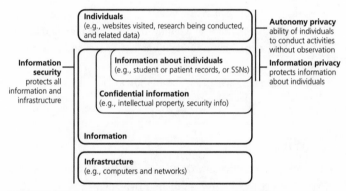

Source: https://security.berkeley.edu/sites/default/files/uploads/SCreport-final.pdf

Figure 1: Domains covered by autonomy privacy, information privacy, and information security.

Privacy Values

The University of California respects the privacy of individuals. Privacy plays an important role in human dignity and is necessary for an ethical and respectful workplace. The right to privacy is declared in the California constitution. Privacy consists of (1) an individual's ability to conduct activities without concern of or actual observation and (2) the appropriate protection, use, and release of information about individuals. The university must balance its respect for both types of privacy with its other values and with legal, policy, and administrative obligations. Thus, the university continually strives for an appropriate balance between:

- ensuring an appropriate level of privacy through its policies and practices, even as interpretations of privacy change over time;
- nurturing an environment of openness and creativity for teaching and research;
- being an attractive place to work;
- honoring its obligation as a public institution to remain transparent, accountable, and operationally effective and efficient; and
- safeguarding information about individuals and assets for which it is a steward.

Privacy Principles

The privacy principles are derived from the UC Statement of Privacy Values and from established privacy principles such as the Organisation for Economic Co-operation and Development (OECD) Guidelines on the Protection of Privacy and Transborder Flows of Personal Data and the Federal Trade Commission (FTC)'s Fair Information Practice Principles. The UC privacy principles are intended to guide policies and practice in conjunction with well-understood information security objectives of protecting the confidentiality, integrity, and availability of information resources.

Members of the university community are expected to

uphold autonomy privacy, which is the ability of an individual to exercise a substantial degree of control over his or her expressions, associations, and general conduct without unreasonable oversight, interference, or negative consequences. Autonomy privacy principles include free inquiry guided by the First Amendment, respect for individual privacy, and the principle of surveillance guided by the Fourth Amendment.

The university is committed to providing individuals with a reasonable degree of control over the collection, use, and disclosure of information about themselves. The following principles provide guidance to the university for incorporating information privacy into its policies and practices: privacy by design, transparency and notice, choice, information review and correction, information protection, and accountability.

Privacy Balancing Process

The Privacy Balancing Process is a tool to guide policy-making and decision-making when competing privacy interests, university values, or obligations exist and for which no statutory provision, common law, or university policy is directly applicable. The balancing process rests on the acknowledgment that protecting autonomy privacy depends on both protecting information privacy and ensuring information security.

The balancing process must expressly consider the parties' interests, benefits, burdens, and consequences associated with the proposed action. Each analysis will differ depending on the action and the interests involved. A "party" in such an analysis may be, or represent, an individual, a community, or the university, recognizing that parties may overlap or that a party may have multiple roles. Among the factors to be considered in privacy analysis are these:

- What are the benefits to each party in successfully asserting privacy interests or a specific policy stance? What are the burdens, impacts, and risks to each party if the proposed action is not taken?
- What alternative approaches, or reasonable privacy protections, might be used in conjunction with the proposed action to make it less intrusive?
- What are the costs, whether in dollars, time, effectiveness, or other metrics?
- What actions have been taken (or could be taken) by each party to protect their own interests?
- What new technologies or processes might mitigate the privacy concerns, now or in the foreseeable future?

RECOMMENDATIONS

The Privacy and Information Security Steering Committee final report made four recommendations:

1. *UC Statement of Privacy Values, UC Privacy Principles, and Privacy Balancing Process.* The University shall formally adopt the proposed UC Statement of Privacy Values, Privacy Principles, and Privacy Balancing Process.

2: *Campus Privacy and Information Security Boards.* Each Chancellor shall form a joint Academic Senate–Administration board to advise him or her, or a designee, on privacy and information security; set strategic direction for autonomy privacy, information privacy, and information security; champion the UC Privacy Values, Principles, and Balancing Process; and monitor compliance and assess risk and effectiveness of campus privacy and information security programs.

3. *Systemwide Board for Privacy and Information Security.* The President shall form a joint Academic Senate–Administration board systemwide to advise him or her, or a designee, on privacy and information security; set strategic direction for autonomy privacy, information privacy, and information security; steward the UC Privacy Values, Principles, and Balancing Process; and monitor their effective implementation by campus privacy and information security boards.

4. *Campus Privacy Official.* Each Chancellor should be charged with designating a privacy official to be responsible for the collaborative development, implementation, and administration of a unified privacy program for the campus. The privacy official shall work closely with the campus's privacy and information security board.

CONCLUSIONS

The framework established by the UC-wide initiative is now being disseminated widely, with implementation beginning across the entire system. At UCLA, implementing this framework has led to increased awareness of privacy issues on campus. The principles have proven useful to address a wide array of privacy-related issues, such as diversity and climate, surveillance, online education and educational analytics, distinctions between public and private uses of information about faculty and students, and the formation of public-private partnerships. During two years of meetings and consultation across the UC system, we found that few universities have taken a holistic approach to privacy and information security. Faculty, administrative, and student concerns all were addressed in this process to develop an integrated model of values, principles, and governance that balances privacy and information security interests. The framework deliberately avoids mention of specific technologies, recognizing that policy, principles, and values must transcend today's technical infrastructures. Rather, we developed a framework that is expected to serve the university well into the future. We offer this holistic framework as a model for other universities and institutions of higher education.

NOTES

1. The three authors are members of the UCLA Board on Privacy and Data Protection and were members of the University of California Privacy and Information Security Steering Committee. Christine L. Borgman is professor and presidential chair in information studies at UCLA and a member of the EPIC board of directors. Kent Wada is UCLA's chief privacy officer. James F. Davis is vice provost for information technology and chief academic technology officer at UCLA. This article reflects the work of the UC Privacy and Information Security Steering Committee and Working Group, whose many members are listed on the final report.

ROBOT-SIZED GAPS IN SURVEILLANCE LAW

Ryan Calo

The past several years have seen a renewed interest in robotics, including by lawmakers. More than a dozen states have one or more robot-specific laws on the books.[1] One of the issues lawmakers are concerned about is privacy. Thus, several states now limit how public or private entities may use drones for surveillance.

That robotics would raise privacy concerns is hardly surprising: robots implicate privacy practically by definition. Robots differ from previous and constituent technologies such as laptops precisely in that they proactively explore the physical world.[2] But, owing to the inability of lawmakers and courts to think more broadly about robotics as a technology, emerging law creates or fails to close certain gaps in privacy law.

First, officials tend to define the issue of robotic surveillance too narrowly. State drone laws, for example, look largely to the Federal Aviation Administration's definition of drones as "unmanned aircraft systems." According to the FAA, "an

Ryan Calo is an assistant professor at the University of Washington School of Law and an affiliate scholar at the Stanford Center for Internet and Society.

unmanned aircraft is a device that is used, or is intended to be used, for flight in the air with no onboard pilot."[3]

Robots do not have to fly to observe us. Existing robots can climb the sides of buildings or jump thirty feet into the air onto a roof. There is a robot camera, marketed to police, that spins or rolls around a room in order to create a detailed, 360-degree view in seconds. There are robots in development designed to squeeze under doors. Other systems emulate or even co-opt insects in order to bring cameras or microphones within range of a surveillance target without detection. Current drone bills or laws would not touch the use of such devices by police.

Second, courts have missed or avoided the question of how drones, let alone other robots, would interact with privacy law. In *United States v. Jones*, the Supreme Court held that police needed probable cause to affix a GPS device to a car for the purpose of continuous, long-term surveillance.[4] The decision characterized the action of attaching a device to a car as a trespass, which in turn triggered the Fourth Amendment warrant requirement. Drones would not need to trespass in order to follow a car or person around continuously in public.[5]

In *Florida v. Jardines*, the Supreme Court held that an officer needed probable cause to bring a drug-sniffing dog onto the defendant's porch.[6] While citizens tacitly consent to an officer approaching their door to ask questions, they do not consent to that officer bringing an instrumentality of surveillance up their walkway. Again, the defendant won, but on a theory tying Fourth Amendment protection to an "intrusion" on citizen property. Setting aside the 40 or so percent of Americans who live in apartment complexes with common hallways, or brownstones without front lawns, *Jardines* does not prevent a drone equipped with a chemical sensor from flying near a property.[7]

The gap here is wider yet: *Jardines* actually cements the decades-old holding that citizens do not enjoy a reasonable expectation of privacy in contraband. Period. Imagine if a drone or driverless car circulated throughout a city, mindful of property lines, and autonomously searched homes and people for signs of drugs or weapons. (The relevant sensor technology—thermal imaging, backscatter, and particulate detectors—is all available and dropping in cost.) Imagine further that the robot only alerted police when it detected contraband with sufficient certainty, immediately deleting any image it did not need as evidence so that no human would ever see it.

I realize, of course, that *Kyllo v. United States* suggests that scanning the home with technology not in ordinary use requires a warrant.[8] The core issue in *Kyllo* was that officers could see something *other than* illegal marijuana—infamously, the hour in which the lady takes her sauna. The robot I am imagining here is not a person; it is like a dog that smells everything but only reports apparent violations of the law to human police officers. I submit that courts are as likely to analyze the imagined activity under the contraband line of cases that culminate in *Jardines.*

So, what is the problem exactly? As an analytic matter, the fact that states regulate drones does not preclude them from regulating other robots. That courts protect citizens against trespass does not preclude an interpretation that is more protective—a point Justice Sotomayor makes expressly in her concurrence in *Jones.*

The problem has to do with political capital and judicial habit. Drones have managed to capture the public imagination.[9] Citizens are not going to protest each and every robotic technology that police adopt. Drones created a narrow policy window that closes day by day as citizens acclimate to this transformative technology.

The Supreme Court's decisions, meanwhile, are pyrrhic to a degree: they protect the defendant while reinforcing a narrow interpretation of the Fourth Amendment. *Jones* stands for the proposition that you have a reasonable expectation of privacy in public to the extent that officers trespass on your property—or, maybe, use your own electronic devices to follow you. *Jardines* stands for the proposition that you do not tacitly consent to an officer approaching your door with a dog. If the justices agreed upon anything in *Jardines* it is that you continue to enjoy no reasonable expectation of privacy in contraband.[10]

The purpose of this series is to present a vision of contemporary privacy law. I would see statutes or doctrines that confronted robotics as a common phenomenon. Rather than address mobile, autonomous surveillance technologies piecemeal, officials and courts should think through the sea change that is underfoot. Great work is under way that outlines how privacy law could catch up to surveillance technology without a net loss to certainty or analytic rigor.[11] Society should look to this literature now, as we stand knee deep in waters that will only rise.

NOTES

1. See Ryan Calo, "Robotics and the New Cyberlaw," 103 Cal. L. Rev. (forthcoming 2015).

2. Although there is no consensus definition of a robot, a plurality of commentators think of robots as machines capable of sensing the world, processing what they sense, and acting upon the outcome of that processing. Ibid.

3. Federal Aviation Administration, "Unmanned Aircraft Operations in National Airspace System," 14 CFR Part 91 (February 6, 2007).

4. *United States v. Jones*, 132 S. Ct. 945 (2012).

5. Five of nine justices in *Jones* worried aloud about the prospect of continuous surveillance even in the absence of a physical trespass. These justices spoke in terms of "electronic surveillance," suggesting they had in mind cell phones or preloaded GPS capability, rather than an embodied robot such as a drone.

6. *Florida v. Jardines*, 133 S. Ct. 1409 (2013).

7. The drone could fly near the property line or high enough above the dwelling so as not to implicate the target's property rights. Cf. *Florida v. Riley*, 488 U.S. 445 (1989) (holding that flying over a property with a helicopter is not a search for purposes of the Fourth Amendment) and *United States v. Causby*, 328 U.S. 256 (1946) (abrogating the common-law rule that individual property rights extended indefinitely upward).

8. *Kyllo v. United States*, 533 U.S. 27 (2001).

9. See Ryan Calo, "The Drone as Privacy Catalyst," 64 Stan. L. Rev. Online 19 (2011).

10. Justices Alito, Kennedy, and Breyer, and Chief Justice Roberts, all would have found against the defendant anyway, despite the purported intrusion onto his property.

11. E.g., David Gray and Danielle Citron, "The Right to Quantitative Privacy," 64 Minn. L. Rev. 62 (2013).

PROTECTING SEXUAL PRIVACY IN THE INFORMATION AGE

Danielle Citron

Technological change is at the heart of much information privacy law. Recall privacy law's beginning. In 1890, Samuel Warren and Louis Brandeis, then law partners, wrote "The Right to Privacy" in response to the emerging privacy vulnerabilities of their era. Then, snap cameras and the penny press enabled intrusions into the "sacred precincts of the home." Unwanted disclosures of "domestic intimacies" produced mental distress far greater than physical harm, they argued, warranting law's protection of the "right to be let alone." Courts and legislatures soon followed suit, redressing privacy harms.

Another era's technologies spurred the next major wave of privacy laws: the computer "databanks" of the mid to late twentieth century. Businesses, government, and direct-mail companies amassed digital records on millions of Americans. Those "Big Brother" databases produced widespread panic. From 1965 to 1974, nearly fifty congressional hearings and reports investigated a range of data privacy issues, including the use of census records, access to criminal history records, and the monitoring

Danielle Citron is the Lois K. Macht Research Professor and professor of law at the University of Maryland School of Law.

of political dissidents by the military and law enforcement. In 1973, the secretary of the Department of Health, Education, and Welfare called for a code of Fair Information Practices (FIPs) providing procedural safeguards against technology's potential abuse. FIPs are at the heart of the Fair Credit Reporting Act, the Privacy Act of 1974, the Gramm-Leach-Bliley Act of 1999, the Children's Online Privacy Protection Act, and the Health Insurance Portability and Accountability Act.

Stalking was another hazard of computerized dossiers. In 1989, a deranged fan murdered actress Rebecca Schaeffer after obtaining her home address from California motor vehicle records. The following year, California criminalized stalking. Within five years, all fifty states had adopted stalking statutes.

At the turn of the twenty-first century, advances in digital recording prompted bans on video voyeurism. In 2003, New York passed Stephanie's Law, which makes it illegal to use a device to secretly record or broadcast a person undressing or having sex when that person has a reasonable expectation of privacy. The statute is named for Stephanie Fuller, whose landlord secretly taped her using a camera in the smoke detector above her bed. The federal Video Voyeurism Prevention Act of 2004 makes it a crime to "intentionally capture an image of a private area of an individual without their consent and knowingly do so under circumstances in which an individual has a reasonable expectation of privacy." The statute applies to images captured on federal property.

The law needs updating again to combat destructive invasions of sexual privacy facilitated by networked technologies. Consider the case of Ian Barber, who allegedly posted his ex-girlfriend's nude photos on Twitter and sent them to her employer and sister. New York prosecutors charged him with aggravated harassment, which bans harassing communications sent directly to victims. A judge dismissed the charges because the man had not sent the nude photos to the victim. New York is not an outlier.

Many state harassment and stalking laws require proof that the defendant directly communicated with victims. But with today's technologies stalkers can terrorize victims without ever contacting them. Today social media, blogs, and e-mail are used to torment victims. Tomorrow it may be robots or drones. Stalking and harassment laws should be revised to cover any means, methods, or technologies exploited by perpetrators to stalk and harass victims.

In most states, including New York, it's not a crime to disclose someone's nude photos knowing that the person meant the photos to be kept private. Such nonconsensual pornography, known also as "revenge porn," is a serious form of harassment and often a form of domestic violence. Victims are routinely threatened with sexual assault, harassed, fired from jobs, forced to change schools, even compelled to change their names. Some victims have committed suicide.

Nonconsensual pornography should be a crime. Seven states have banned revenge porn. Seventeen others are considering anti–revenge porn legislation, as is Congresswoman Jackie Speier, who is drafting a sexual privacy bill. Time will tell whether Congress and states like New York respond to sexual privacy invasions.

Some object to criminalizing invasions of sexual privacy because free speech will be chilled. That's why it is crucial to craft narrow statutes that only punish individuals who knowingly and maliciously invade another's privacy and trust. Other features of anti–revenge porn laws can ensure that defendants have clear notice about what constitutes criminal activity and exclude innocent behavior and images related to matters of public interest.

Even so, some argue that revenge porn laws are doomed to fail because nonconsensual pornography does not fall within a category of unprotected speech. To criminalize revenge porn, they say, the court would have to recognize it as a new category of unprotected speech, which it would not do. Another argument is that even if law could secure civil remedies for revenge porn, it could not impose criminal penalties because the First Amendment treats criminal and civil laws differently. These objections are unfounded and deserve serious attention lest they be taken seriously.

Let's first address the argument that revenge porn laws are unconstitutional because they do not involve categorically unprotected speech like true threats. Advocates rely on *United States v. Stevens*, which struck down a statute punishing depictions of animal cruelty distributed for commercial gain. In *Stevens*, the court rejected the government's argument that depictions of animal cruelty amounted to a new category of unprotected speech. As the court explained, the First Amendment does not permit the government to prohibit speech just because it lacks value or because the "ad hoc calculus of costs and benefits tilts in a statute's favor." The court explained that it lacks "freewheeling authority to declare new categories of speech outside the scope of the First Amendment." The court did not say that only speech falling within explicitly recognized categories (such as defamation, true threats, obscenity, imminent incitement of violence, and crime-facilitating speech) are proscribable. To the contrary, the court specifically recognized that other forms of speech have "enjoyed less rigorous protection as a historical matter, even though they have not been recognized as such explicitly."

Disclosing private communications about purely private matters is just the sort of speech referred to in *Stevens* that has enjoyed less rigorous protection as a historical matter. We do *not* need a new category of unprotected speech to square anti–revenge porn criminal laws with the First Amendment. Now for the cases establishing that precedent.

Smith v. Daily Mail, decided in 1979, addressed the constitutionality of a newspaper's criminal conviction for publishing the name of a juvenile accused of murder. The court laid down the now well-established rule that "if a newspaper lawfully obtains truthful information about a matter of public significance then state officials may not constitutionally punish the publication of the information, absent a need to further a state interest of the highest order." Ever since, the court has refused to adopt a bright-line rule precluding civil or criminal liability for truthful publications "invading 'an area of privacy' defined by the State." Rather the court has issued narrow decisions that specifically acknowledge that press freedom and privacy rights are both "plainly rooted in the traditions and significant concerns of the society."

Consider *Bartnicki v. Vopper*. There, an unidentified person intercepted and recorded a cell phone call between the president of a local teacher's union and the union's chief negotiator.

During the call, one of the parties talked about "go[ing] to the homes" of school board members to "blow off their front porches." A radio commentator, who received a copy of the intercepted call in his mailbox, broadcast the tape. The radio personality incurred civil penalties for publishing the cell phone conversation in violation of the Wiretap Act.

The court characterized the wiretapping penalty as presenting a "conflict between interests of the highest order—on the one hand, the interest in the full and free dissemination of information concerning public issues, and, on the other hand, the interest in individual privacy and, more specifically, in fostering private speech." For the court, free speech interests appeared on both sides of the calculus. The court recognized that "the disclosure of the contents of a private conversation can be an even greater intrusion on privacy than the interception itself." The penalties were struck down because the private cell phone conversation about the union negotiations "unquestionably" involved a "matter of public concern." Because the private call did not involve "trade secrets or domestic gossip or other information of purely private concern," the privacy concerns vindicated by the Wiretap Act had to "give way" to "the interest in publishing matters of public importance."

The state interest in protecting the privacy of communications is strong enough to justify regulation if the communications involve "purely private" matters, like nude images. Neil Richards has argued, and lower courts have ruled, that a lower level of First Amendment scrutiny applies to the nonconsensual publication of "domestic gossip or other information of purely private concern." Appellate courts have affirmed the constitutionality of civil penalties under the wiretapping statute for the unwanted disclosures of private communications involving "purely private matters."

Lower courts have upheld claims for public disclosure of private fact in cases involving the nonconsensual publication of sex videos. In *Michaels v. Internet Entertainment Group, Inc.*, an adult entertainment company obtained a copy of a sex video made by a celebrity couple, Bret Michaels and Pamela Anderson Lee. The court enjoined the publication of the sex tape because the public had no legitimate interest in graphic depictions of the "most intimate aspects of" a celebrity couple's relationship. As the court explained, a video recording of two individuals engaged in sexual relations "represents the deepest possible intrusion into private affairs."

These decisions support the constitutionality of efforts to criminalize revenge porn. Nude photos and sex tapes are among the most private and intimate facts; the public has no legitimate interest in seeing someone's nude images without that person's consent. On the other hand, the nonconsensual disclosure of a person's nude images would assuredly chill private expression. Without any expectation of privacy, victims would not share their naked images. With an expectation of privacy, victims would be more inclined to engage in communications of a sexual nature. Such sharing may enhance intimacy among couples and the willingness to be forthright in other aspects of relationships.

When would victims' privacy concerns have to cede to society's interest in learning about matters of public importance? Recall that women revealed to the press that former congressman Anthony Weiner had sent them sexually explicit photographs of himself via Twitter messages. His decision to send such messages sheds light on the soundness of his judgment. Unlike the typical revenge porn scenario involving private individuals whose affairs are not of broad public interest, the photos of Weiner are a matter of public import, and so their publication would be constitutionally protected.

Another way to understand the constitutionality of revenge porn statutes is through the lens of confidentiality law. Revenge porn is a "legally actionable breach of confidence." Confidentiality regulations are less troubling from a First Amendment perspective because they penalize the breach of an assumed or implied duty rather than the injury caused by the publication of words. Instead of prohibiting a certain kind of speech, confidentiality law enforces express or implied promises and shared expectations.

Now for the view that civil revenge porn remedies might stand but that criminal penalties cannot because the First Amendment has different rules for them. Generally speaking, the First Amendment rules for tort remedies and criminal prosecutions are the same. Eugene Volokh has said that the court has "refused invitations to treat civil liability differently from criminal liability for First Amendment purposes." In *New York Times v. Sullivan*, the court explained, "What a State may not constitutionally bring about by means of a criminal statute is likewise beyond the reach of its civil law." As the court recognized, the treatment is the same though the threat of civil damage awards can be more inhibiting than the fear of criminal prosecution and civil defendants do not enjoy special protections that are available to criminal defendants, such as the requirement of proof beyond a reasonable doubt.

It's worth noting Volokh's view that "the vagueness doctrine may be more in play in criminal cases than in civil cases (compare *FCC v. Pacifica Foundation* and its stress on absence of criminal liability); a *mens rea* of recklessness or worse may be required for criminal liability in public concern libel cases (by analogy to *Gertz v. Robert Welch*'s holding about punitive damages)." He states (and I agree): "I don't think that the revenge porn statutes that I've seen suffer from vagueness problems."

These myths should be seen and understood for what they are: misleading and uninformed. If we are going to oppose efforts to curtail revenge porn, let's be honest about why. Opponents may reject them on policy grounds. They can worry that it is a bad idea to criminalize revenge porn. They can insist it is no big deal. Let the discussions on the merits begin.

PRIVACY OPPORTUNITIES AND CHALLENGES WITH EUROPE'S NEW DATA PROTECTION REGIME

Simon Davies

From the perspective of many U.S. policy makers and rights advocates, the pace of domestic reform in the arenas of privacy, security, and accountability since the Snowden revelations has been significant. Commitments by the White House to curb mass surveillance by security agencies and proposals for improved legal protections and enhanced transparency and security by corporations are widely hailed as a substantial win for privacy.

This perspective is not universally reflected in Europe. There, leading politicians and privacy regulators have consistently attacked the United States over what they believe is general inactivity over privacy reforms. This view has contributed to what is perhaps the greatest surge in privacy reform in Europe's history.

In early 2014, the EU's privacy supremo, Isabelle Falque-Pierrotin—president of the French privacy watchdog CNIL (the National Commission on Informatics and Liberty) and chair of Article 29 (the European confederation of data protection

Simon Davies founded Privacy International in 1990, and served as director general until 2012.

authorities)—expressed concern that President Obama had done little to alleviate concerns in Europe over U.S. surveillance.

"At some point European citizens and the European data protection authorities want facts—not only intentions, good will or propositions—they want facts. And as far as the facts are concerned, we are not satisfied as European data protection authorities in the way data from EU citizens are collected."

Falque-Pierrotin's views are not unique. The Obama administration's much-heralded reform program for the NSA is viewed by many in the European community as a disappointment. While offering some notable concessions to the U.S. rule of law, it provides almost no brake on the global surveillance operations engineered by the NSA over the past sixty years. Although Obama has devoted a surprisingly large chunk of his public statements to overseas sentiments, there is a persuasive concern in the EU that he has offered little more than a PR strategy to allay the concern of government leaders.

Obama's comprehensive speech early in 2014 skirted the issue of overseas data collection. It referred only to the possibility of exploring options to limit retention periods for that data. This omission signaled that the global data collection apparatus will remain intact, a reform gap that did not escape the attention of EU politicians.

While constantly referring to the sanctity of "ordinary citizens" (presumably declared "ordinary" after the fact of collection), Obama chose to focus on protections for the heads of friendly governments:

> Given the understandable attention that this issue has received,
> I have made clear to the intelligence community that—unless

there is a compelling national security purpose—we will not monitor the communications of heads of state and government of our close friends and allies.

While U.S. privacy advocates are right to conditionally welcome some of Obama's reforms, the silence from the United States over collection of data from non-U.S. persons has fueled support for strengthened legal protections over the collection and processing of data on EU citizens.

The negative perception of U.S. attitudes toward the privacy of Europeans is not confined to security operations. Indeed there's a widespread view among policy makers that none of the U.S. administrations from Clinton onward have delivered on commitments to reform the arenas of privacy and surveillance at the international level.

Safe Harbor, for example—a legal device used to ensure that the data trade could continue between Europe and the United States after the 1995 EU Data Protection Directive was passed— was generally viewed as a minimalist solution that was supposed to evolve into something stronger. It transpired, however, that the United States never intended to follow through on commitments to strengthen it. Even now, when the stakes are at an all-time high in terms of transatlantic privacy arrangements, the United States continues to alarm EU law reformers by refusing to agree to substantial reform of the mechanism.

There can be little doubt that the overall temperature over privacy and surveillance has reached an unprecedented level in the United States over the past year, but with regard to the benefit to EU persons, Falque-Pierrotin and other privacy leaders in Europe interpret this dynamic as activity rather than outcome.

This perception has contributed to an unprecedented shift toward stronger privacy protections in Europe, and a hardening of the overall policy position regarding data collection and processing by the United States. Over the past year the so-called Transatlantic Divide on privacy between the United States and Europe has widened significantly. This shift could indicate new dynamics in the global push on America to institute more meaningful privacy safeguards for non-U.S. persons.

In this short period the European Parliament and the European courts have created strengthened protections that will place further pressure on the U.S. administration to make ongoing efforts to respect individual rights at a global level.

First, the European Court of Justice has overturned an EU directive that had required service providers to store communications data on all their customers. While the long-term implications are still unclear, this is a significant strike against mass surveillance that will have global repercussions for service providers and for law enforcement and security agencies.

The decision declared: "Untargeted, suspicionless data retention is too broad and not limited to the absolute minimum necessary." This position essentially rules out any data retention and limits possible law enforcement activities to case-by-case activities rather than mass retention of entire populations.

Second, the European Parliament has almost unanimously passed a new data protection framework that strengthens privacy and information rights and will force overseas-based companies to respect those rights. Until recently the fate of this legislation was unclear, with many of its provisions twisting in the wind under intense controversy.

The position taken by the EU Parliament provides testimony

of just how far attitudes toward privacy reform have recently evolved. At the beginning of 2014, when the Irish presidency of the European Council commenced its six-month term, the future of data protection reform looked bleak. In January 2014 an unprecedented barrage of lobbying across the economic spectrum rolled into play with the intention of generating so many amendments that the regulation would be hopelessly compromised. Then the World Economic Forum released a report calling for a "rethink" on privacy. In March 2014 the council started drafting a report that would devastate huge chunks of the reforms in the regulation. By April the UK government was telling the rest of the world—including India and Southeast Asia—that it should take a pragmatic view of data protection legislation. This trend has reversed.

Most recently, Europe's highest court determined that there exists a "right to be forgotten" that places an obligation on search companies and other data companies such as Google to respect people's wishes to have certain types of identifiable information removed.

Finally—although not directly related to privacy—the parliament last month approved strong net neutrality provisions, indicating a much more positive and informed position on a spectrum of key online issues.

There has also been a string of national court decisions that strengthen sovereign control and rights over online activities, including a UK ruling requiring Google to face its litigants on British territory and a German decision that Facebook is subject to its national data protection law.

It's perhaps premature to suggest that these developments will create a sea change in relations between the two regions, but with developments in the free trade agreement and data transfer arrangements such as the Safe Harbor agreement in the balance, there's an overall expectation that the United States should create genuine reform efforts. In the post-Snowden era such thinking is becoming institutional.

The EU election produced a new parliament with a markedly different political composition than the past one. This, however, should not be misinterpreted by the United States as a future easy ride on privacy issues. A more Euro-skeptic parliament may result in a stronger emphasis on sovereign protections. That situation could open a Pandora's box for U.S.-European relations.

PSEUDONYMS BY ANOTHER NAME: IDENTITY MANAGEMENT IN A TIME OF SURVEILLANCE

A. Michael Froomkin

Identity management looms as one of the privacy battle-grounds of the coming decade. The very term is contested. In its most minimal form it means little more than sharing and keeping secure track of login credentials, passwords, and other identity tokens. The more capacious version envisions an "identity ecosystem" in which people's tools carefully measure out the information they reveal, and in which we all have a portfolio of identities and personae tailored to circumstances. What is more, in this more robust vision, many transactions and relationships that currently require verification of identity move instead to a default of only requiring that a person demonstrate capability or authorization.

A privacy-protective identity management architecture matters because the drift toward strong binding between identity and online activities enables multiple forms of profiling and surveillance by both the public and private sectors. Moving to a

A. Michael Froomkin is the Laurie Silvers & Mitchell Rubenstein Distinguished Professor of Law at the University of Miami in Coral Gables, Florida, specializing in Internet law and administrative law.

better system would make a substantial part of that monitoring and data aggregation more difficult. Thus, a privacy-protective identity management ecosystem has value on its own or as a complement to a more comprehensive reform of privacy protection, whether EU-style or otherwise. Importantly, given present trends, a reformed ID ecosystem would protect privacy against private monitoring and against illicit public-sector surveillance also.

In the United States the present and future of privacy seem to fall somewhere between grim and apocalyptic. The NSA seeks to capture all digital data. Law enforcement agencies club together to share surveillance data in fusion centers. Corporate data brokers find new ways to collect and use personal data. Yet, it seems all too likely that data gathering will remain largely unencumbered by EU-style privacy regulation for the foreseeable future. Data privacy is being squeezed by a technological pincer composed of multiple advances in data collection on the one hand and rapid advances in data collation on the other. Big data gets bigger and faster, and is composed of an ever-wider variety of information sources collected and shared by corporations and governments.

The catalog of threats to privacy runs from the capture of Internet-based communications to location and communications monitoring via cell phones and license plate tracking. Effective facial recognition is on the horizon. Both public and private bodies increasingly deploy cameras in public, and process and store the results; increasingly too they share data—or at least the private sector shares with the government, whether willingly or otherwise. Plus, as people become more used to (and more dependent on) electronic social and economic intermediaries such as Facebook, Twitter, Instagram, Amazon, and Google, they themselves become key sources of data that others can use to track and correlate their movements, associations, and even ideas—not to mention those of the people around them.

In an environment of increasingly pervasive surveillance of communications, transactions, and movements, the average U.S. person is almost defenseless. Legal limits on data collection tend to lag technical developments. As regards private-sector collection, the dominant, largely laissez-faire theory of contract means that privacy routinely falls in the face of standard-form extractions of consent. As regards data collection in public and also data use and reuse, First Amendment considerations might make it difficult to outlaw the repetition of many true facts not obtained in confidence. Furthermore, there is relatively little the average person can do about physical privacy in daily life. Obscuring license plates is illegal in most states. Many states also make it a crime to wear a mask in public, although the constitutionality of that ban is debatable. Most cell phones are locked, and rooting them is neither simple nor costless, nor does it make it possible to solve all the privacy issues.

Electronic privacy has for years seemed to be an area where privacy tools might make a significant dent in data collection and surveillance. Unfortunately, cryptography's potential is yet to be realized; disk encryption software now ships as an option with major operating systems, but encrypted e-mail remains a specialist item. Cell phones leak information not just via location tracking but also through the apps and uses that make the devices worthwhile to most users. Estimates suggest that when one counts senders and recipients, one company—Google—sees half the e-mails sent nationally. And we now know beyond a reasonable doubt that the NSA has adopted a vacuum cleaner policy toward both electronic communications and location data.

One of the first papers I wrote about privacy, back in 1995, contrasted four types of communications in which the sender's identity was at least partially hidden. Listed in declining order of privacy protection, they were: (1) untraceable anonymity, (2) traceable anonymity, (3) untraceable pseudonymity, and (4) traceable pseudonymity. Encouraging untraceable anonymity has for years seemed to me to be one of the best routes to the achievement of electronic privacy. "Three can keep a secret if two of them are dead": if people could transact and communicate anonymously, then the exchange would by its nature remain outside the ever-expanding digital dossiers. But even though we have increasingly reliable privacy-enhanced communications through systems like Tor, and even though at least a segment of the public has demonstrated an appetite for semianonymous cryptocurrency (see the Bitcoin fiasco), the fact remains that for most people most of the time, anonymous electronic communication, much less anonymous transactions, are further and further out of reach because tracking and correlating technologies are getting better all the time. Whether due to the use of MAC numbers to track equipment, cookies and browser fingerprints to track software and its users, or cross-linking of location data with other data captures, be it phones, faces, loyalty cards, or self-surveillance, the fact is that anonymity is on the ropes even before we get to the various impediments in the United States—and even more in other countries—to real anonymity.

A focus on identity management involves a shift from

anonymity to pseudonymity. Plus, if one is being realistic about the legal environment, any robust identity management likely will have substantial traceability in it. Useful, attractive identity management tools can only exist if we first create a legal and standards-based infrastructure that supports them. In the United States, at least, the legal piece of that infrastructure will require action by the federal government. Although actors within the Obama administration have signaled support for strong identity management in the National Strategy for Trusted Identities in Cyberspace (NSTIC), not all parts of this administration are speaking in unison. Worse, the early signs are that the NSTIC implementation will fall far short of its potential.

NSTIC is almost unique among recent government pronouncements about the regulation of the Internet domestically.[1] The typical government report on cyberspace is long on the threats of cyberterrorism, money laundering, and (sometimes) so-called cyberpiracy (unlicensed digital copying), and gives at most lip service to the importance of privacy and individual data security. The exceptions are reports on the dangers of ID theft—which seem mostly to stress caution in Internet use rather than secure software—and NSTIC itself. NSTIC envisions an "identity ecosystem" guided by four key values:

- Identity solutions will be privacy enhancing and voluntary
- Identity solutions will be secure and resilient
- Identity solutions will be interoperable
- Identity solutions will be cost-effective and easy to use

These are good goals, and to realize them would be a substantial achievement. Even if it is limited to cyberspace—in other words, even if it does not directly address the problems of surveillance in the physical world—in this list lie the seeds for an "ecosystem" based on enabling law and voluntary standards that could very substantially enhance data privacy by allowing people to compartmentalize their lives and by creating obstacles to marketers and others stitching those compartments together.

The problem that NSTIC could solve is that without some sort of intervention the interests of marketers, law enforcement, and (in part as a result) hardware and software designers alike most frequently tend toward making technology surveillance-friendly and toward making communications and transactions easily linkable. If we each have only one identity capable of transacting, and if our access to communications resources, such as ISPs and e-mail, requires payment—or even just authentication—then all too quickly everything we do online is at risk of being joined to our dossier. The growth of real-world surveillance, and the ease with which cell phone tracking and face recognition will allow linkage to virtual identities, only adds to the potential linkage. The consequences are that one is, effectively, always being watched as one speaks or reads, buys or sells, or joins with friends, colleagues, coreligionists, fellow activists, or hobbyists. In the long term, a world of near-total surveillance and endless record-keeping is likely to be one with less liberty, less experimentation, and certainly far less joy (except maybe for the watchers).

Robust privacy-enhancing identities—pseudonyms—could put some brakes on this totalizing future. But in order for identities to genuinely serve privacy in a new digital privacy ecosystem, these roles need to have capabilities to transact, at least in amounts large enough to purchase ISP and cell phone services. And we need standards that ensure our hardware does not betray our identities: using different identities on the same computer or the same cell phone must not result in the easy collapse of multiple identities into one. Thus, given the current communications infrastructure, computers and phones must have a way of alternating among multiple identities, down to the technical (MAC, IPv6, and IMEI number) level.

In its most robust form, we would have true untraceable pseudonymity powered by payer-anonymous digital cash. But even a weaker form, one that built in something as ugly as identity escrow—ways in which the government might pierce the identity veil when armed with sufficient cause and legal process—would still be a substantial improvement over the path we are on. It is possible to imagine the outlines of a privacy-hardened identity infrastructure that fully caters to all but the very most unreasonable demands of the law enforcement and security communities. In this ecosystem, we would each have a root identity, as we do now, and we would normally use that identity for large financial transactions. In addition, however, everyone would have the ability to create limited-purpose identities that would be backed up by digital certificates issued by an ID guarantor—a role banks, for example, might be happy to play. Some of these certificates would be "attribute" certs, stating that the holder is, for example, over eighteen, or a veteran, or a member of the AAA for 2015. Others would be "capability" certs, much like credit cards today, stating that the identity has an annual pass to ride the bus or has a credit line to draw on. (There could be limits on the size of the credit line if there are money-laundering concerns, although several banks already offer the option of throwaway credit card numbers for people concerned about using their credit cards online; those cards, however, carry the name of the underlying cardholder, while in a privacy-enhanced ID system they would not need to.) We might define a flag that distinguished between personae that are anchored to a real identity and those that are not; the anchored ones would deserve more trust, even if we didn't know who was behind them.

In time, we would learn to interact online through virtualized compartments—configurable personas. Doing so would enable a stricter, cryptographically enforced separation between work, home, and play. It would also provide for in-depth defense against identity theft—if someone, say, broke into one's Facebook persona, the attacker wouldn't be able to leverage this to the work persona. Furthermore, there would be less need for tight security controls imposed at work to limit (or monitor) private personae—already an increasing problem with corporate-issued cell phones and laptops.

Even this—a much watered-down recipe for limited privacy—is a tall order in today's United States. It is hard enough to persuade even democratic governments of the virtues of free speech, and even harder to find any enthusiasm for the freer speech that comes from strong pseudonyms. When one gets to the even freer speech that comes from untraceable anonymity, governments get cold feet—and when money is involved, the opposition is only stronger.

The Obama administration's National Strategy for Trusted Identities in Cyberspace (NSTIC) raised hopes that the U.S. government might swing its weight toward the design of legal and technical architectures designed to simultaneously increase online security while reducing the privacy costs increasingly imposed as a condition of even access to online content. At present those hopes have yet to be realized. There is much to be done.

NOTES

1. The caveat is important: the U.S. government often seems more willing to talk of anonymization on the Internet as a potentially empowering tool for dissidents abroad than for citizens at home.

TAKING THE LONG WAY HOME: THE HUMAN RIGHT OF PRIVACY

Deborah Hurley

Queen Elizabeth I passed a law in 1571 mandating that all male commoners in England must wear a woolen cap. The queen had good reason for this early Renaissance industrial policy. It was enacted to protect the English knitting industry and to provide employment for the people.

This rule may seem quaint today, one of the sweeping, imperious edicts from the era of absolute monarchy. Yet, is it not possible to imagine an upcoming regulation, Off with Their Hats!, barring the near-ubiquitous baseball cap and other brimmed hats so that facial recognition technology will not be frustrated in its efforts to capture digital images and measurements of every face?

Another tough leader, Theodore Roosevelt, shouted into the throng at Madison Square Garden a century ago, "Friends, perhaps once in a generation, perhaps not so often, there comes a chance for the people of a country to play their part wisely and

---

Deborah Hurley is the principal of the consulting firm she founded in 1996, which advises governments, international organizations, nongovernmental organizations, and foundations on advanced science and technology policy.

fearlessly in some great battle of the age-long warfare for human rights."

Go suit up. Privacy is a human right.

The Universal Declaration of Human Rights (UDHR), the founding document of the modern human rights era, was adopted by the United Nations General Assembly in 1948 without a single dissenting vote. We do not know the words of wisdom that Theodore Roosevelt gave his niece Eleanor along with his arm to escort her down the aisle. Whether or not human rights were mentioned on her wedding day, Eleanor took up TR's challenge and played her part wisely and fearlessly when the opportunity arose. Eleanor Roosevelt chaired the UDHR drafting committee.

The UDHR, along with the International Covenant on Civil and Political Rights (ICCPR) and the International Covenant on Economic, Social and Cultural Rights, both from 1966, are called the International Bill of Human Rights. The International Bill of Human Rights is one of the most successful legal regimes in the history of the world. More than 160 countries are parties to these conventions. The adoption and ratification of the main human rights instruments by so many nations underscore the high degree of international consensus on the principles of human rights.

Human rights were considered so important that governments extraordinarily agreed to limit their own sovereignty, reallocating some of their power to other nations and international bodies and some to individuals. Human rights conventions limit the range of a country's discretion regarding individuals within their geographic territory. Not only are individuals acknowledged as the basis of governmental authority, but individuals may also reach outside their nation to seek redress for human rights violations by their governments.

Along with rights to life, liberty, equal protection under the law, and presumption of innocence, privacy is a human right. UDHR article twelve proclaimed, and ICCPR article seventeen, almost twenty years later, repeated, "No one shall be subjected to arbitrary interference with his privacy, family, home or correspondence, nor to unlawful attacks on his honour and reputation. Everyone has the right to the protection of the law against such interference or attacks." The ICCPR entered into force in 1976 and the United States ratified the treaty in 1992. The United States has since submitted four periodic reports.

Continually over sixty-five years, the human right of privacy has been declared, protected, and affirmed in treaties, national constitutions, regional regulations, and national legislation on every continent. The United States catalyzed modern human rights protection. The human rights instruments and institutions, along with their implementation and enforcement, guarantee human rights.

Privacy and protection of personal information support autonomy, self-determination, and dignity. On the wind these days flies the canard that privacy is an amorphous concept. This gossamer attack, that it is not clear what privacy actually is, generates a miasma of doubt.

On the contrary, the protection of privacy is deeply embedded in the laws and institutions of the modern democratic state. Moreover, one has a strong visceral sense of privacy and apprehends clearly when it has been abrogated. It would be like saying that an individual does not understand liberty, freedom, and justice. Yet, while passersby on the sidewalk might be hard-pressed to give a textbook definition of privacy, they could easily provide several examples of violations of their privacy, together with severe real-world consequences of job loss, public humiliation, and damage to reputation. Just because privacy is a concept, rather than a wrench, does not render it any less valuable to us. Love is another one of those abstract concepts in which we place deep, abiding value.

Traditionally, U.S. law recognized four invasions of privacy: intrusion on the right to be let alone, public disclosure of private facts, depiction in a false light, and commercial appropriation of personal information. Modern data protection and privacy laws contain core elements, sometimes described as "Fair Information Practices," that set out the rights and responsibilities associated with the collection and use of personal data.

Each individual must own and control her personal information.

A quarter-century after the UDHR, the United States was continuing to set the global pace for protection of personal data and privacy. As the era of mass computerization dawned, the United States recognized the potential to collect and manipulate vast troves of personal data. The United States adopted the 1974 Privacy Act and encouraged the adoption around the world of rules to protect personal data and privacy. So began an impressive roll call, continuing through the succeeding decades to the present, of laws and enforcement institutions. Today, over one hundred countries have data protection and privacy legislation. Not only is protection of privacy and personal data widespread, but also there is broad agreement about the principles that undergird the modern right of privacy.

Yet, the U.S. progenitor became the outlier of this forty-year-strong global trend. The 1974 Privacy Act covered part of the federal public sector. As information and communication technologies advanced with uptake throughout society, other countries adopted and amended data protection and privacy legislation to include the private sector and the rest of the public sector. The United States did not keep up with these developments, with the result that Americans have less protection for their personal data than people in many other nations. It is ironic that U.S. companies, which operate in countries with broadly based data protection and privacy laws, provide a higher level of personal data protection for residents of those countries than they do for the personal data of Americans. The festive, baton-waving grand marshal of the privacy parade let the band march ahead and fell to the back, trying to look inconspicuous. But its bright red, white, and blue uniform makes it impossible to hide as it brings up the rear in gluttonous isolation, guzzling personal information, increasingly feared and resented. As an example, in the United States, medical information is the high-value haul of the data brokers. It is bought, sold, and traded among the medical establishment, insurers, employers, companies, and anyone else with the meager means to purchase it.

Human rights are universal, indivisible, interdependent, interrelated, and inalienable. In this palace with many chambers, one human right is not superior to any other. That being said, for me privacy is a gateway human right, which facilitates other human rights, such as freedom of movement and freedom of association, vital for political discourse and religious worship.

Just as we guard against measures that have a chilling effect on speech, so too should we worry about chilling effects on civic participation, discourse, and association when each individual's every act is exposed to the glare of bright lights and, to compound the agony, the individual has no control over or knowledge of her personal information's creation, collection, use, or purpose of use, and who else will see it and in what context. What if people hesitate to communicate due to concerns about invasive observation of their movements, relationships, and affiliations, even of personal information outside their own awareness, longitudinally over a lifetime? Now, that is chilling.

To the same degree that liberty and freedom are defended from tyranny and oppression, how best to instantiate protection of personal data and privacy, shelter it from inevitable forces of depredation, and deploy the mutually reinforcing means of laws, technological design, standards, and norms? There already exists a worldwide body of law and institutions. The lag is in implementation and enforcement. This is the easier part of the task, since the legal framework is already in place. As far as additional legislation, clearly the biggest change would come from U.S. adoption of comprehensive federal legislation to protect personal data and privacy, a welcome return to a leadership role. India already has a bill. Its passage would bring over one billion people under the privacy protection umbrella. China presents a harder case, but the prize of another billion people makes it an attractive challenge.

Similarly, privacy-enhancing technologies abound. But, repeatedly, when a technical development team receives functionality criteria, privacy is omitted. Include privacy in specifications and designers will deliver it. Privacy and security standards, such as the ISO 27001 series and many others, provide guidance. There are social and economic norms, a number of which have already been mentioned.

Already breaching the shore comes the next technological tidal wave, the Internet of Things. The ubiquitous information environment will include computing everywhere, inorganic and organic, in solids, liquids, and the air one breathes. Some inhaled devices will stay to reside, others will ride out on the exhale. In the era of ingestibles, implantables, and individual-specific nutriceuticals, the human aspect will matter more than ever. With the nascent big data already collected, it is evident that it may be surpassingly difficult to maintain anonymity, remain de-identified, and avoid re-identification. It becomes ever more important that the individual have control of her personal data.

Much of this information activity will happen outside the limits of human sensory and temporal awareness. No matter. A patient unconscious in a hospital bed is entitled to the same suite of rights and level of privacy protection as if she were going about her daily life.

And so at the end we come back to where we began and to what we have known all along. Privacy is a human right. Each government, company, and individual, as well as all other non-state actors, has an affirmative duty to safeguard it. The protection exists. The hard work is done. But there are severe lapses in implementation and enforcement. Privacy is important for the individual and, arguably, even more vital for the democratic community and its maintenance of vibrant, robust civic participation and social and economic discourse. The locus of ownership and control of personal information must lie with the individual. Technology can reinforce and actualize this principle. As personal information proliferates and becomes ubiquitous, the need to adhere to this standard becomes increasingly acute.

> *And the end of all our exploring*
> *Will be to arrive where we started*
> *And know the place for the first time.*
>   —*Four Quartets*, T.S. Eliot

ACCOUNTABILITY UNCHAINED: BULK DATA RETENTION, PREEMPTIVE SURVEILLANCE, AND TRANSATLANTIC DATA PROTECTION

Kristina Irion

INTRODUCTION

The innovations on which today's Internet proliferated have been a major gift from its founders and the U.S. government to the world. Ever since the rise of the Internet it has attracted utopian ideas of a free and borderless cyberspace, a man-made global commons that serves an international community of users. First commercialization and now the prevalence of state surveillance have significantly depreciated the utopian patina.

The Internet's borderless nature, which was once heralded as rising above the nation state, has actually enabled some states to rise above their borders when engaging in mass surveillance that affects users on a global scale. International human rights law and emerging Internet governance principles have not been authoritative enough to protect users' privacy and the confidentiality of communications.[1]

Kristina Irion is assistant professor at the Department of Public Policy and Research Director, Public Policy, with the Center for Media and Communications Studies (CMCS) at Central European University.

More or less openly, Western democracies embarked on the path of mass surveillance with the aim of fighting crime and defending national security. Although country-specific approaches vary, reflecting political and ideological differences, mass surveillance powers frequently raise issues of constitutional compatibility. Beyond striking a balance between public security and privacy, systemic surveillance carries the potential to erode democracy from the inside.[2]

This chapter's focus is on the safeguards and accountability of mass surveillance in Europe and the United States and how these affect transatlantic relations. It queries whether national systems of checks and balances are still adequate in relation to the growth and the globalization of surveillance capabilities. Lacking safeguards and accountability at the national level can exacerbate transnational surveillance. It can lead to asymmetries between countries that are precisely at the core of the transatlantic rift over mass surveillance. The chapter concludes with a brief review of proposals for how to reduce them.

FROM TARGETED TO MASS SURVEILLANCE

As a transcendent technology, communications permeates every aspect of contemporary life because it satisfies humans' need to socialize and connect with others. Apart from the actual content of electronic communications, metadata[3] and log files are routinely available by-products, which can be used to reconstruct the circumstances of a communications event. The framework for the state's legitimate interferences with communications content and metadata is called "lawful" interception authority, which can be further broken down into intelligence and law enforcement powers.

Due to various technical and ideological leaps, surveillance capabilities could expand exponentially. Wiretapping electronic communications has become low-hanging fruit since it is now technically feasible to access, copy, store, and analyze large amounts of electronic communications. Moreover, Internet traffic does not conform to the political geography offline; instead the topography of cyberspace gravitates toward Western countries, in particular the United States. At neuralgic points, such as core infrastructure and popular online services, international communications are especially exposed to wiretapping.[4]

Against the backdrop of counterterrorism and the fight against crime surveillance, ideology appears to have morphed with technological determinism, where feasibility determines strategies. The two new strategies that have been added to the arsenal of "lawful" interception are preemptive monitoring[5] and bulk data retention.[6] Both aim at whole populations of inconspicuous users, which marks a quantitative and qualitative shift away from targeted surveillance.

On both sides of the Atlantic, this trend is reflected in the passing of legislation that authorizes transnational surveillance, notably the 2008 U.S. FISA Amendments Act[7] and the national intelligence laws of the UK, Sweden, France, and Germany.[8] From what has been revealed by international news media, the United States and the UK are believed to engage in the large-scale upstream collection of electronic communications while the other countries may not command comparable capabilities as of yet.[9]

NEW SURVEILLANCE MEETS
ACCOUNTABILITY STANDARDS

In its 2013 resolution "The Right to Privacy in the Digital Age," the United Nations General Assembly affirms that fundamental rights apply undiminished online, including the right to privacy.[10] Mass surveillance constitutes a particularly serious interference with the right to privacy, notwithstanding if it is actually taking place or a lingering threat as long as individuals form an impression of surveillance. Privacy has a supporting function for the exercise of other fundamental rights and collective freedoms, notably the freedom of speech and assembly, which jointly underpin the functioning of democracy.

Democracies' respect for fundamental rights would already dictate substantive boundaries curtailing surveillance powers and complementary safeguards against excesses and abuse thereof. As a recent report from the Center for European Policy Studies explained, "It is the purpose and the scale of surveillance that are precisely at the core of what differentiates democratic regimes from police states."[11]

Moreover, state actions are situated within the chain of democratic legitimization, which is the reason for insisting on a precise surveillance mandate but also for ex post facto measures to hold competent authorities accountable for their actions. Together, the protection of fundamental rights and democratic accountability make a strong argument for claiming that at the national level surveillance should be nested in rigorous checks and balances.

Every country has its unique system of constitutional protections, safeguards, and due process requirements that surveillance measures have to comply with. However, these arrangements evolved in the context of targeted surveillance of limited capacity, with intelligence work being a secretive affair conducted under equally closed oversight mechanisms.[12] Without significant modifications, mass monitoring has been fitted inside these arrangements, although the circumstances are to an appreciable extent different.

Preemptive and systemic surveillance exceeds qualitatively and quantitatively the situation of targeted surveillance. It is incumbent upon the states that issued these new powers to revise these mandates to correspond with national constitutions and international human rights law. The 2014 NETmundial multistakeholder meeting resolved that

> procedures, practices and legislation regarding the surveillance of communications, their interception and collection of personal data, including mass surveillance, [. . .] should be reviewed, with a view to upholding the right to privacy.[13]

This would involve revisiting taken-for-granted intelligence paradigms, such as secrecy, discretionary powers, and national security exemptions,[14] to name just a few, in relation to large-scale surveillance programs.

Ultimately, the legitimacy of electronic surveillance is increasingly intertwined with the classical set of checks and balances associated with government accountability. The 2013 resolution of the United Nations General Assembly calls on states to

> establish or maintain existing independent, effective domestic oversight mechanisms capable of ensuring transparency, as ap-

propriate, and accountability for state surveillance of communications, their interception and collection of personal data.[15]

States are responsible for devising safeguards that would afford a measure of transparency, supervision, and accountability commensurate with the dangers of the state's interference in fundamental rights and the risks for democratic institutions.

TRANSPARENCY

At the most basic level, transparency is certainly appropriate with regard to the statutes that should afford clarity on the scope, boundaries, and consequences of surveillance powers.[16] However, it is often not possible to infer from the legal mandate this information with certainty without accessing accompanying but classified interpretations.[17] In many instances, the exact meaning of surveillance authorities remains largely abstract to the public, unless they make headlines that would convey a more accessible account.

The flip side of legal certainty is that generalized terms in statutes may actually not contain surveillance powers but involuntarily facilitate their expansion. Bigo et al. state that

> law-making has not kept pace with the technological developments seen in surveillance practices in recent years, often designed for traditional intelligence techniques such as wiretapping.[18]

Transparency is a prerequisite of accountability, and where it is not mission-critical, the cloak of secrecy that covers entire electronic surveillance programs by national intelligence should be lifted.[19] The knowledge about the mere existence of blanket surveillance schemes is not equally as compromising as it would be for targeted actions. To the contrary, democratic societies should rethink the contours of secrecy, because the public sacrifice to national security must be transparent to its constituency.

A principle flowing from both due process and Fair Information Practices is that individuals should be informed when access to their data has been given to intelligence services.[20] What should be uncontroversial is the release on an annual basis of statistical data about electronic surveillance that provides accessible and meaningful information about its scope, scale, origin, and effects.

SUPERVISION

At the national level, supervision of surveillance powers is also not static but an evolving concept that has already been responsive to emerging needs. For example, parliamentary and/or judicial oversight of the activities of national intelligence agencies is now widely accepted, but for some countries this is a relatively recent development.[21] Local arrangements of supervision are very diverse but have certain structural elements in common, such as a combination of internal and external oversight with a link to democratic accountability. The efficiency of external supervision mechanisms remains a matter of concern, often due to a lack of independence, competences, resources, and even information.[22]

Additionally, large-scale electronic surveillance calls for new directions in supervision that are cognizant of compliance with relevant data protection standards. The assembly of EU data protection authorities considers that

> an effective and independent supervision of intelligence services implies a genuine involvement of the data protection authorities. [...] This [oversight] should include fully independent checks on data processing operations by an independent body as well as effective enforcement powers.[23]

Even where data protection authorities will not play the envisaged role, oversight has to extend to the systems and schemes used for data collection and processing in electronic communications surveillance.

Independent judicial oversight and access to justice continue to make inroads toward upholding the rule of law in the context of electronic surveillance. Aside from national courts, the two top European courts, in Strasbourg (European Court of Human Rights) and Luxembourg (Court of Justice of the European Union), quite frequently now decide on instruments of electronic surveillance. Their respective case law covers preemptive surveillance and the retention of communications metadata, with two more cases pending concerning electronic mass surveillance in Sweden and the UK.[24] Both courts stress the role of "adequate and effective guarantees against abuse" and "substantive or procedural conditions" that would limit the interference with fundamental rights to what is necessary and proportionate.

ACCOUNTABILITY

Accountability is valid currency in government and privacy protection, interests that converge in state surveillance of electronic communications. At an institutional level, accountability requires that an organization take appropriate and effective measures to ensure internal compliance with relevant laws and procedures. For authorities competent to conduct electronic surveillance, assuming internal accountability should be an evident consequence of deriving their mandate from statutes. However, accountability cannot be treated as an internal affair but must be demonstrated and verifiable if necessary. Hence, accountability is linked to internal checks and external supervision.

With a view to accountability, there are some striking parallels between independent regulatory agencies, such as energy regulators and central banks, and those national authorities competent to conduct electronic surveillance. In both cases, there is a delegation of competences from the state to an authority that enjoys a special status vis-à-vis the government, which requires a more sophisticated setup to protect the status and mandate of the agency while ensuring that in their operations they remain accountable to the public interest, the national constitution, and democracy at large.

In democracies, through general elections governments can be held accountable to the citizens, including for the extent of state surveillance. Admittedly, democratic accountability is a broad concept in which issues of surveillance compete with other salient policies. Nonetheless, surveillance touches upon a principle relationship between the state and the citizens, which in some countries may become a premise for parties' ideological differentiation. For a global user community, democratic accountability cannot be achieved, except indirectly via the proxy of the local electorate.

TRANSATLANTIC SURVEILLANCE ASYMMETRIES

Over the last decade, EU-U.S. relations have been probed by transnational surveillance in a variety of areas.[25] The 2013 revelations in international news media about U.S. and UK electronic mass surveillance programs as well as a flourishing transatlantic intelligence cooperation reached a new climax. While national security is not part of its remit, the EU finds itself in the difficult position of having to defend the fundamental rights of European citizens against U.S. surveillance in a context where several EU member states, such as the UK, Sweden, France, and Germany, are implicated in mass surveillance to varying degrees.[26]

EU institutions are particularly alarmed by the massive violation of European citizens' fundamental rights through the suspected unfettered surveillance of electronic communications.[27] Interpretations of the U.S. FISA section 702 powers come to the conclusion that it permits the warrantless interception of international communications during transit through the United States and the targeting of non-U.S. persons reasonably believed to be located outside the United States.[28] However, several EU member states, for example Germany, Sweden, and the UK, follow a similar approach.[29]

The distinction between domestic and international communications is a legacy of telecommunications, when this was a straightforward exercise. The political geography was ingrained in the public switched telephony network, but this is no longer the case with decentralized Internet traffic. By maintaining the distinction between domestic and external communications, national surveillance could subtly expand in scope with mass surveillance capabilities adding scale. In practice, this distinction is hard to sustain, which calls into question the rationale of keeping it intact.[30]

This leads to a key difference between the United States and Europe, i.e., regional human rights with supranational oversight by an international court.[31] The European Convention on Human Rights protects the privacy of the correspondence of everyone in the territory of a member state of the Council of Europe. The European Court of Human Rights, based in Strasbourg, reviews the compatibility of member state actions with the convention, and its jurisprudence on domestic surveillance laws offers a rich framework of reference on their legality.[32] By contrast, Europeans have no agency to protect them from U.S. surveillance.

EU politics is now exploring a wide array of strategies that would reestablish the respect for European citizens' fundamental rights online at various levels. In several fora the transatlantic dialogue continues with the aim of entering into bilateral agreements and reviving the EU-U.S. Mutual Legal Assistance Agreement (MLAA). International law, however appealing, may not bring about the desired change for the simple reasons that it would have little to add to existing international human rights law and that national security exceptions may prove highly resistant.

At the EU level, the general data protection framework

restricts the transfer of personal data originating in the EU to nonmember countries, which, under the risk of electronic surveillance, may be further restricted to prohibit passing on personal data for the purpose of national security. This would primarily create a conflict of law on the part of the organizations processing such data, for example in the context of business. There are also various initiatives that explore the feasibility of European services capable of evading U.S. surveillance, such as certified e-mail services, EU preferential routing, and European cloud legislation, among others.

Outside politics, the loss of trust in Internet communications and services develops its own dynamic in which public- and private-sector organizations are increasingly risk-averse. If government cloud computing makes a good indicator, then organizations change strategies in acquisition of IT services with a view to avoiding the legal risks of foreign intelligence gathering.[33] There are also signs that Internet users are increasingly open to privacy-enhancing technologies, such as anonymous browsing and encryption. When diplomacy has no leverage to tame surveillance, the real pressure is economic.

NOTES

1. See UN News Center, "General Assembly backs right to privacy in digital age," December 19, 2013; NETmundial, "NETmundial Multistakeholder Statement," São Paulo, Brazil, April 24, 2014.
2. The European Court of Human Rights (ECtHR) observes that "a system of secret surveillance for the protection of national security may undermine or even destroy democracy under the cloak of defending it." See *Gabriele Weber and Cesar Richard Savaria v.*

Germany, ECtHR no. 54934/00, decision of June 29, 2006, para. 106. Cf. D. Bigo et al., "Mass Surveillance of Personal Data by EU Member States and Its Compatibility with EU Law," study for the European Parliament (Brussels: European Union, 2013), 5, 14.

3. In U.S. terminology metadata is called "call-detail records" (CDR); in the EU metadata is referred to as "traffic data."

4. Cf. Bigo, et al., "Mass Surveillance of Personal Data," 20; C. Bowden, "The U.S. surveillance programmes and their impact on EU citizens' fundamental rights," study for the European Parliament (Brussels: European Union, 2013), 13f.

5. Preemptive monitoring concerns the collection of electronic communications or related data according to fairly broad parameters with a view to subsequent analysis intended to detect dangers for national and/or public security.

6. Bulk data retention is a method of data preservation over a certain period of time so that it is thus available for retroactive investigations into electronic communications by competent authorities.

7. U.S. Congress, Foreign Intelligence Surveillance Act of 1978 Amendments of 2008, 122 Stat. 2436, Public Law 110–261, section 702.

8. For a list in order of estimated magnitude, see Bigo et al., "Mass Surveillance of Personal Data," 19f.

9. Ibid.

10. UN General Assembly, "The Right to Privacy in the Digital Age," resolution adopted at the sixty-eighth General Assembly on December 18, 2013, 4(d).

11. Bigo et al., "Mass Surveillance of Personal Data," 5.

12. Regarding EU member states, see Article 29 Working Party, Opinion 04/2014 on Surveillance of Electronic Communications for Intelligence and National Security Purposes, adopted on April 10, 2014, 9f.; Bigo et al., "Mass Surveillance of Personal Data."

13. NETmundial, "NETmundial Multistakeholder Statement."

14. According to the Article 29 Working Party, "there is no automatic presumption that the national security argument used by a national authority exists and is valid. This has to be demonstrated." Article 29 Working Party, Opinion 04/2014, 6.

15. UN General Assembly, "The Right to Privacy in the Digital Age," 4(d).

16. In Europe, following the ECtHR, "foreseeability" is a prerequisite quality of the law; see *Weber and Savaria v. Germany*, paragraphs 84ff.; *Case of Liberty and Others v. the United Kingdom*, no. 58243/00 (ECtHR, judgment of July 1, 2008), paragraphs 66–67.

17. For example, in the absence of an authoritative interpretation of the surveillance powers, legal accounts of the powers under section 702 of the 2008 FISA amendment are often vaguely dismissed as wrong or exaggerated. See for example U.S. Mission to the EU, "Five Myths Regarding Privacy and Law Enforcement Access to Personal Information in the EU and the US" (2012).

18. Bigo et al., "Mass Surveillance of Personal Data," 25.

19. For European standards, the resistance against data retention laws resembled class actions: 11,128 Austrians filed a lawsuit, cf. *Digital Rights Ireland and Seitlinger and Others*, Joined Cases C-293/12 and C-594/12 (CJEU, judgment of 8 April 2014); against the German data retention law, 34,939 individuals went to court, cf. BVerfG, 1 BvR 256/08 (German Federal Constitutional Court, judgment of March 2010), BVerfGE 125, 260.

20. Article 29 Working Party, Opinion 04/2014, 2.

21. Bigo et al., "Mass Surveillance of Personal Data," 13.

22. Ibid., 26.

23. Article 29 Working Party, Opinion 04/2014, 8.

24. *Weber and Savaria v. Germany, Case of Liberty and Others v. the United Kingdom, Digital Rights Ireland and Seitlinger and Others.* Pending: *Centrum för rättvisa v. Sweden*, 35252/08 (ECtHR, application of July 14, 2008); *Big Brother Watch and others vs. the*

United Kingdom, 58170/13 (ECtHR, application of September 4, 2013).

25. For example the global satellite interception system ECHELON, the US-VISIT-related extraction of passenger name records in air transport, and the exploitation of SWIFT data under the U.S. Terrorist Finance Tracking Program.

26. Bigo et al., "Mass Surveillance of Personal Data," 27.

27. See "European Parliament resolution on the U.S. National Security Agency surveillance programme, surveillance bodies in various Member States and their impact on EU citizens' privacy," 2013/2682(RSP), July 4, 2013.

28. Bowden, "The U.S. surveillance programmes and their impact," 19; K. Irion, "International Communications Tapped for Intelligence-Gathering," *Communications of the ACM* 52, no. 2 (February 2009): 26.

29. Bigo et al., "Mass Surveillance of Personal Data," 22.

30. Ibid.

31. Irion, "International Communications Tapped for Intelligence-Gathering," 28. NB: The EU Charter of Fundamental Rights does also afford the fundamental rights to privacy and to data protection for everyone; however, member states' surveillance laws fall outside EU authority and thus review mechanisms.

32. See notes 16 and 24.

33. K. Irion, "Government Cloud Computing and the National Data Sovereignty," *Policy and Internet* 4, no. 3 (2012): 40–41.

THE SURVEILLANCE SOCIETY AND TRANSPARENT YOU

Jeff Jonas

THE IRRESISTIBLE SURVEILLANCE SOCIETY

A surveillance society is inevitable and irreversible. More interestingly, I believe a surveillance society will also prove to be irresistible. This movement is not only being driven by governments; it is being driven primarily by consumers—you and me—as we eagerly adopt ever-increasing numbers of irresistible goods and services, often not knowing what personal information is collected or how it may ultimately end up being used. Given that this is the journey we are on, now is the time to embrace Privacy by Design (PbD) principles as we create the new sensors, technologies, and systems of tomorrow.

Surveillance itself is not necessarily bad. The word *surveil* basically means "to look." Before you cross the street you use surveillance to determine when it is safe to cross. Surveillance is one of the means by which we are informed—an essential element to better decision-making. While crossing the street, people use their eyes and ears to collect data as they assess traffic conditions. Much like pedestrians, organizations collect data to assess opportunity and risk, as well. People rely on surveillance

---

Jeff Jonas is an IBM Fellow and chief scientist of context computing.

to survive, similar to the way organizations rely on surveillance to compete.

Of course, some surveillance is bad: when it is illegal, breaks contractual agreements, or falls outside of social norms. Most people would agree that using a flying quad-copter with a video camera to secretly record a couple's private picnic is not good surveillance. Similarly, organizations that covertly collect information from consumers without notice and customer consent would be exhibiting bad behavior.

Fortunately, most organizations are not covertly collecting information. This is because they don't have to. As luck would have it, the majority of consumers don't even read terms of use. The more irresistible the product, it seems, the greater the consumer's indifference to its terms of use. Check out the terms of use in your free e-mail service one of these days if you want proof—look for language like "the service provider is granted a worldwide license to use, reproduce, modify, communicate, and publish your content." Companies providing free products (e.g., e-mail, social networking, storage, picture portfolio hosting) are viable business concerns only because of what they are able to learn, and their freedom of action to benefit from what they learn (e.g., targeted advertisements).

Organizations of all types and sizes are quickly recognizing they too must have access to more information and attempt to make sense of it all—if they hope to remain competitive (and in business). The more organizations look for data, the more surveillance they employ.

EVER-WIDENING OBSERVATION SPACES

For a moment, think about the net sum of an organization's information as its available "observation space." Then as an organization dreams up new information worth acquiring, think about this as the process of "widening observation spaces."

Prioritizing what information to wish for next is driven by interest in (a) finding new customers; (b) better serving existing customers; (c) reducing risk, e.g., fraud detection; or (c) other efficiencies, e.g., better fleet routing to reduce fuel consumption. Interestingly, most organizations are not even making use of all the data they already have in hand. Accordingly, the first place an organization looks for more information is internally. Eventually, though, many organizations come to a point where they feel the information they need next is external.

Buying information from data aggregators is a long-standing regular business practice for widening the observation space. Credit reporting agencies were some of the first, if not the first, to sell widely available aggregated data. Laws like the Fair Credit Reporting Act (FCRA) then followed. The FCRA is one of the better privacy laws in the United States; unfortunately this type of consumer protection remains narrowly limited to credit reporting agencies. Today, there are a substantial number of organizations amassing data that are not subject to any FCRA-like consumer protections. And yet we are only on the cusp of even more surveillance and more information sharing. Two big new emerging trends come to mind: (1) the Internet of Things (IoT); and (2) the dynamics by which your friends hand over your personal data, casually and inadvertently.

The IoT is in its infancy—cell phones being an early example.

Then along came cars with real-time tracking systems that also allowed others to unlock your car remotely from space via satellite (circa 2000). Fast-forward. Today, we see things like thermostats and bathroom scales reporting into big databases in the sky. Coming soon, the combination of these environmental sensors will reveal not only that you are home, but also how long you are in the kitchen—at the stove versus over the sink. These discussions are happening now as related to valuable new products and services (e.g., monitoring an independently living elderly person for life safety: they are now in bed for the night but have left the stove on!).

As consumers adopt more irresistible products, they hand over more and more personal information. Organizations delivering this business are the ones getting smarter. This is a self-reinforcing loop. The good news is that if an organization collects information from you directly, they will be sure to put you on notice . . . and you will probably consent (as you check that checkbox without a glance at the small print). The bad news: often, getting more personal information about you does not even require giving you notice. Third parties are readily providing your information. One simple example is property ownership, which is a public record. A more subtle third-party source of information about you is your friends. Let's say you are my close friend and I have provided you with my public and private e-mail addresses and phone numbers. You have recorded these in your electronic address book for quick reference. Then unbeknownst to me, because you never called and asked, you loaded your address book up into five to ten social networking sites—some you like and continue to use, and other sites you found of no use and have since abandoned. Do you think you can list every such site where you have consented to uploading your address book? Most people cannot.

Of course, well-behaved social media sites will ask before they upload your address book. At the same time, some of these same sites make it exceptionally hard to benefit from their system without giving up your whole address book first. If you try to connect with a specific person on a social network site, you will find many of these sites provide no mechanism to enter one e-mail address or cell phone number at a time. Instead they say, "Import all contacts? Click here to accept." For good reason, your entire address book is exceptionally valuable to them. While I recommend resisting, most folks do not. As a result, your name, e-mail addresses, phone numbers, and more likely exist in tens if not hundreds of different computer systems.[1] If you attempted to locate all of the instances of your information, you would fail. Your information is out there . . . and it is a runaway on the lam.

As the IoT and secondary parties generate new volumes of data about you, this information will have a tendency to pool into centralized databases. Many benefits come from centralized information, ranging from better predictions (from the more complete picture) to greater cost-effectiveness (because centralized data is generally cheaper than lots of distributed databases). The fast adoption of cloud computing—where many of these large centralized databases are emerging—is happening for exactly this reason: it's smarter and cheaper. This explosion of pooled information about you is going to make it exceptionally hard to hide things in the future. You are becoming more transparent, whether you like it or not.

TRANSPARENT YOU

Often the term "transparency" is used to describe how public the activities of an organization are (for example, the procedures and rulings of the U.S. Foreign Intelligence Surveillance Act [FISA] court). Across the board, transparency is on the rise. While government agencies, especially in recent years, are revealing more to the public about their activities, you too are steadily becoming more and more transparent to others—and at an even faster pace. The ability of a company—a company that you have no relationship with—to know where you live, your demographics, your interests, and how to contact you is unprecedented.

As more irresistible goods and services are increasingly integrated into your house and personal effects, much of this information about you will end up residing in centrally integrated databases owned and controlled by others. In the future secrets will become harder to maintain—your secrets and everyone else's secrets too.

WHAT NEXT?

More information is going to be collected. More information is going to flow. And you yourself are likely to be driving this forward, fast—because the personal benefits will appear to outweigh any harm. In terms of more surveillance, where we are going is where we are going. So now what?

On the macro scale, hope for strong democratic processes, oversight, and accountability. Hope for leaders and institutions that we can trust. There is plenty to be done on this front, globally.

On the micro scale, one thing that can be done is the implementation of Privacy by Design (PbD), which includes but is not limited to Privacy Enhancing Technologies (PETs).[2] Whether one is envisioning a new class of sensors, smarter algorithms, or novel products, this is the time to think about ways to design systems that reduce future misuse or harm. Pencils, for example, are generally used for good. But every now and then a bad person uses a pencil to make evil plans. That's not a reason to prohibit the use of pencils. Nonetheless, one day it was discovered lead caused harm, so pencils are now made with graphite, not lead. These pencils serve the same utility, yet are engineered to reduce harm. In the area of IoT, big data, and analytics, here are some examples of PbD:

Tamper-Resistant Audit Logs

Sometimes referred to as "immutable audit logs," these audit logging systems record events in a manner that cannot be altered—even the database administrator cannot hide his or her actions. Let's say law enforcement has lawfully collected some information around an investigation; however, someone has asked the database administrator to search for records related to his ex-wife. Each such search is recorded in a tamper-resistant audit log. Despite the database administrator's privileged access, he is unable to erase the footprints of his own unauthorized search. Later, when determining if someone has abused their privileges, this evidence will be plain as day when the folks from accountability and oversight show up to investigate.

Information Transfer Accountability

If an organization is going to transfer information from one system to another, it should do so in a manner in which the source system remembers which records were transferred, to where, and when. Many systems keep track of where each of their records has came from, but few systems record what exactly they sent elsewhere. With such a feature, an organization would be able to help consumers fully understand where their data has been sent. Imagine if a bank provided a screen detailing with whom they have shared any of your details. Something like this exists today. At the bottom of your credit report there is an inquiries section. This section contains a list of organizations that have had access to your credit report in recent months.

PII Attribute Anonymization[3]

Often an organization has to take personally identifiable information (PII) from one system, reorganize it, copy it to another system, and then combine it with some other information. For example, an organization might want to combine its employee data with its fraud data to weed out employee corruption. Doing this involves moving these two piles of data into a new central pile. Unfortunately, for every additional copy of the data one makes, the greater the risk of misuse. One remedy for this involves first anonymizing the individual PII attributes (e.g., name, date of birth, and Social Security) before they are transferred along to another system. Such techniques permit an organization to still perform analytics while at the same time greatly reducing the risk of unintended disclosure.[4] The advantage being, if this database of anonymized PII gets compromised, such anonymized PII data is much less useful to the adversary.

Data Expiration and Annotated Tails

There is some discussion about the idea that consumers should have the "right to be forgotten"—essentially giving consumers the ability to escape their past. One remedy put forward involves allowing consumers to ask search engine providers to suppress certain search results about them. One set of alternatives to this might be data expiration and annotated tails. Some data could have standard, preset durations (e.g., arrest records) that uniformly benefit all. Consumers already enjoy these proven benefits thanks to the Fair Credit Reporting Act (FCRA), which requires credit reporting agencies to remove negative information from their search results after a set time period (e.g., bankruptcy records no longer appear in your credit report after ten years). For data not subject to expiration or records not yet expired, consumers could be given the right to annotate their records (a.k.a. annotate their tails). This too has been seen to be effective in the FCRA law where a consumer can post a consumer statement (e.g., explaining some late-paid bills as an exception due to a one-time family member medical emergency). Whether laws come into force allowing consumers to suppress search engine results or not, engineering in (to systems and processes) support for such things as data expiration and annotated tails could add benefit.

While these are merely four Privacy by Design ideas, be assured, there are endless opportunities just waiting to be envisioned and explored. But why bother?

WHY BOTHER?

Some might wonder why we should take any action at all to build better systems when consumers and organizations are working together so diligently to instrument and analyze the world around us. A good question, but consider this:

- Many organizations believe consumers at least care in the abstract, and that consumers may in time come to prefer privacy-protective brands.
- Many organizations believe that regulators care and that they have a reason to care about regulators.
- Privacy-protective technologies can have secondary benefits as well, e.g., offering consumers access and correction rights to their information can result in more complete and more accurate information.
- Some privacy-enhancing technology will also play an important role in brand protection, e.g. reducing the risk of unintended disclosures (losing customer data) and the bad press that often accompanies such events.

One more practical tip: it seems that the adoption of privacy-enhancing technology is faster if it is baked in and included in the price of a product than if it is sold as a stand-alone.

IN CLOSING

Ubiquitous sensors and exceptionally smart analytics are going to transform what is computable; competitive business pressures combined with consumers' voracious appetite for new, irresistible services will continue to drive this charge. As we envision this future world and dream up next-generation sensors and computing platforms, now is this time to bake in Privacy by Design principles. In our emerging surveillance society we are living longer and healthier lives than at any time in the history of mankind. And with some forethought the systems that take us there will cause less harm.

NOTES

1. And if you include backup copies, your information easily exists in thousands of locations.
2. As discussed in Executive Office of the President, "Big Data: Seizing Opportunities, Preserving Values," May 2014.
3. Note: The goal of this technique is not de-identification, as every record can be re-identified because each record has a pointer to its original record. For this reason, don't confuse PII attribute anonymization with "de-identification" techniques. De-identification is used when one is trying to permanently hide the identity associated with a record. This, by the way, is tricky business, as has been proven by academics. And lightly de-identified data, when matched up against tertiary data sources, has proven to be rather easy to re-identify (recovering, with some certainty, who is who). Heavily de-identified data that makes re-identification near impossible may at the same time lose a degree of utility.
4. While producing materially similar results.

ANONYMITY AND REASON

Harry Lewis

I s there a right to anonymous speech? Should there be?

Courts have found that, under some circumstances, the First Amendment entails a right to express oneself without being identified. In its 1995 *McIntyre* decision, the U.S. Supreme Court found that citizens have a right to distribute anonymous political literature, overturning a local ordinance to the contrary. The court used a sweeping justification grounded in the Bill of Rights:

> Protections for anonymous speech are vital to democratic discourse. Allowing dissenters to shield their identities frees them to express critical minority views [...] Anonymity is a shield from the tyranny of the majority [...] It thus exemplifies the purpose behind the Bill of Rights [...]: to protect unpopular individuals from retaliation ... at the hand of an intolerant society.

Seen from such a high altitude, the right to anonymous speech springs from the same source as the secret ballot in U.S.

Harry Lewis is the Gordon McKay Professor of Computer Science at Harvard University.

elections. Protecting the right to express unpopular views outweighs any right to identify the speaker. The court's decisions that political contributions are a form of speech entitled to anonymity are consistent with *McIntyre*, even though some individual justices saw the cases differently.

Forms of expression that are protected in political contexts are not invariably accepted as protected equally in other contexts. It took until 1973 (in *Miller v. California*) for the Supreme Court to establish clearly that pornography was, in general, entitled to the same First Amendment protection as political leaflets. Or perhaps what the court found was that almost any speech act could be political, so almost all should receive the same protections. Either way, it took a couple of centuries for the protections for political speech to be extended to speech that would generally be considered apolitical.

Anonymous speech is in the midst of a similar evolution of standards. Anonymous garbage, we might say, is morally equivalent to pornography—perhaps of limited social value and certainly harmful sometimes, and yet generally not unlawful. Under the bargain encoded in the Bill of Rights, the risks of excessive speech control are worse than the risks of harmful speech. So citizens are left to decide for themselves what to see, read, and listen to.

What film forced to the surface in the 1970s for the right to edgy forms of expression, Internet blogs and comment sections are forcing to the surface today for the right to anonymity. Now as then, Americans are putting their First Amendment rights to less-than-honorable use—as Justice Scalia said in his dissent in *McIntyre*, anonymity "facilitates wrong by eliminating accountability, which is ordinarily the very purpose of the anonymity."

And now as then, legislatures and public moralists are trying to strike back.

So it is that representatives to the legislature of the state of New York in 2013 introduced an "Internet protection act," an amendment to civil rights law protecting not any right to speech or to anonymity on the Internet, but a novel "right to know who is behind an anonymous internet posting." A similar bill was introduced in Illinois (the Internet Posting Removal Act).

So it is that Gary C. Woodward, a communications studies professor at the College of New Jersey, stated, "As a culture we seem to be forgetting that attaching names to opinions is part of living in a civil society. It's a fraudulent kind of rhetoric that keeps sources in the shadows." True perhaps, but the same thing could be said about the results of any election in which citizens go to the polls wearing neither donkey nor elephant pins. "Some people right here in my neighborhood," one might say, "are responsible for electing that turkey. And the cowards won't identify themselves!"

The deeper rationale for the American tradition of protecting anonymity is far older than the Bill of Rights. Since the Renaissance, Justitia has been blind, because she listens to arguments impartially, regardless of who is making them. Indeed, respect for anonymous speech stems from the Enlightenment program itself, the notion that ideas should be founded on verifiable facts and reasoned argumentation. Government by the people rests on the faith that citizens can figure out what is best for them without instruction by superior authorities.

Anonymous communication played a crucial role in the American Revolution. In January of 1776, a long pamphlet was published in Philadelphia. It was "addressed to the Inhabitants of America, on the following subjects: Of the Origin and Design of Government in general, with concise Remarks on the English Constitution; Of Monarchy and Hereditary Succession"; and so on. *Common Sense* was published anonymously because it was treasonous. Thomas Paine would have been put to death by the British authorities had he been identified and captured. But this pamphlet was a publishing sensation. *Common Sense* sold half a million copies in the first year, even though no one knew who wrote it. Without this nameless argument, the revolution might not have gotten the public support it needed to end seven years later in victory for the Americans.

Common Sense was a triumph of persuasion over authority. It was a text that men and women could discuss and argue about. It was designed to stir the emotions, but it was not mere rabble-rousing.

A decade later, the U.S. Constitution was awaiting ratification by the thirteen newly independent states. Three of the great men of the early republic wrote essays, now referred to as the Federalist Papers, arguing for adoption of the Constitution. They authored these as "Publius," borrowing the name of a Roman who had been instrumental in overthrowing the monarchy and founding the Roman Republic. They began by setting their objective even higher than arguing for the Constitution. The question, they said, was about reason itself.

[I]t seems to have been reserved to the people of this country, by their conduct and example, to decide the important question, whether societies of men are really capable or not, of establishing good government from reflection and choice, or whether they are forever destined to depend, for their political constitutions, on accident and force.

The authors chose to write anonymously not out of fear, as Paine had done when he wrote *Common Sense*. They were respected public figures, and the war was over. They chose to write anonymously so that their argument would carry through force of reason rather than through exercise of authority. Masking their identities *strengthened* their argument. By writing collectively under a Roman pseudonym, the authors were able to speak as generic citizens of the republic. But at a deeper level their use of anonymity was an appeal to human reason. An argument for empowering ordinary people resistant to hereditary authority was more credible because it was anonymous and the actual authority of the authors was not revealed.

That is anonymity at its best: the words themselves making their case, not the speaker. A modern confirming experiment was the reaction when prolific Wikipedia editor Adrianne Wadewitz decided to drop her genderless pseudonym. "Oh, you're a woman" or "You can't really be a woman" or "You don't write like a woman," her fellow Wikipedians complained. "All of a sudden my arguments were not taken as seriously or were judged as hysterical or emotional," she reported.

Anonymity is the enemy of authority, including authoritarian governments in the Middle East. Facebook was a powerful organizing and information dissemination tool during the Arab Spring, used to announce antigovernment rallies and to aggregate news reports of government outrages. But Facebook is a real-identity site and risked becoming a tool of the regime. The problem was resolved by having important protest pages owned by real people in the United States who secretly conveyed their login credentials to people in the war zone, but the technology that made the site so accessible and powerful also made it vulnerable.

So anonymous speech remains important to this day as a tool of fearful nonconformists and antiauthoritarians. Anonymity needs to be defended for the same reasons as ever: to protect the speech rights of those with unpopular views.

But some online anonymous speakers are cowards with no real need for protection and simply want to hide while being bullies and trolls. Anonymous speech without a reasoned foundation lacks credibility. Journalism writer Dan Gillmor has a credibility scale on which he places various forms of media. On his scale, anonymous comments have negative credibility. The right thing to do is not to take them as possibly true or possibly false, but to treat them as false until proven otherwise.

By Gillmor's principle, should the colonists have been skeptical of Paine's tract? Certainly. The genius of *Common Sense* is that it was persuasive. It moved the reader from negative to positive along the credibility scale.

If words are food for the mind, then lazy, cowardly, anonymous online speech needs to be regarded as worse than empty calories—something more like a potential poison.

Of course online speech is not going to come with nutrition labels. Facebook "likes" and Google plus-ones are crude attempts to create nutritional value tags on speech. But should we trust the collective judgment of button clickers who are only indicating that they "thumbs-up" something? More nuanced, Wikipedia-style vetting systems for online comments are emerging, but such tools have a long way to go.

In fact, the battle for anonymity is being carried on in code as well as in law. Not every system that is designed, with good reason, to *authenticate* users need also *identify* users, but the two concepts are commonly engineered together, as though they were inseparable. Protection of online anonymous speech will require that authentication systems not reveal their users' identities except, perhaps, under carefully stipulated conditions.

In the meantime, it is the responsibility of educated people, trained in the art of critical thinking, to be skeptical and to teach others to be skeptical. Cyberspace is full of unedited, low-value content. Children should learn to ignore what is written anonymously online, and to read critically and dispassionately what they actually do read. Honorable people, free people, stand behind their words when they can.

But sometimes they can't. So we can't entirely ignore anonymous speech, because what might we be missing if we did? And yet anything we read affects us, try though we may to be skeptical. In a controlled experiment, opinions of an article depended on the gist of the comments. Readers thought the same article was more positive if the comments were positive than if the comments were negative.

Psychology teaches that, Enlightenment idealism notwithstanding, human beings are not reasoning automata. Their irrational instincts at one time in evolutionary history may have meant the difference between survival and death. Scientifically enlightened, democratic civic institutions have to be run by imperfectly rational beings.

The challenge of anonymous speech in a free society is how cognitively imperfect beings can live by the rule of reason. Among the responsibilities of civic life is to speak in our own voices when we can, and to take anonymous words seriously only if their anonymity is understandable. "Words can never hurt me" is an unfashionable maxim today, because of heightened awareness of bullying and the scars it leaves. But robust discourse on matters of civic importance demands a refusal to be intimidated by shadows and ghosts. Can we, without cutting ourselves off from the richness of social discourse, harden our reasoning apparatus against anonymous garbage and deceptions?

This is a major challenge to democratized speech. How will we know whom to trust when we may not know who anyone is? Without well-developed filters, the rule of reason may give way to the faux democracy of mob rule.

In democracies, the filtering job cannot be assigned to the government. In the United States, anti-anonymity statutes are politically popular but most would, in time, fail the test of constitutionality. Only citizens themselves can be trusted to determine what to ignore and what to take seriously. Anonymity is too important to give up—but the next generation has to be taught how to live with it.

CRYPTOGRAPHY IS THE FUTURE

Anna Lysyanskaya

Over the last year, we have heard quite a bit of debate about whether, as a society, we should be comfortable with giving up our privacy—the privacy of our call records, of our on-line transactions, of our comings and goings—in order to allow agencies such as the NSA to track terrorists, or simply because we live in a digital world in which privacy must be sacrificed for convenience or other important goals.

We would actually do better by asking a different question, namely: how can law enforcement agencies track terrorists without harming the privacy of law-abiding citizens? More generally, how can we gain the benefits of the digital age without sacrificing privacy? At least in theory, this is possible to do. At first, I am going to focus on the NSA because if we need not sacrifice privacy even to track terrorists, we surely do not need to sacrifice privacy for all the other reasons we are given! I am not going to speak of drawing legal boundaries around what the government can and cannot do; instead, I would like to draw attention to a wealth of technological solutions that, given such legal boundaries, would guarantee that law enforcement and

Anna Lysyanskaya is a professor of computer science at Brown University.

national security programs cannot do anything that goes outside of them.

For example, in one shocking revelation, we learned that several phone companies have supplied the NSA with the entirety of the call records of their customers. One reason that the NSA requested all these records, even though they are really interested in only a few of the entries, is because the identities of their targets must be kept secret to ensure they do not learn of the government's interest in them, and the NSA does not trust the phone companies to keep them secret. Although the NSA collects all of this data, our government tells us that NSA analysts can only query information pertaining to individuals who are linked to terrorist suspects by a certain number of hops according to a process that is laid out in FISA court orders. Everything else is supposed to be kept private—but this requires that we trust the government to safeguard these vast treasure troves of personal data.

Yet, there is no need for us to have to trust the government to protect our data. The NSA analysts could have acquired exactly the same information—namely, the phone records of their target individuals and those linked to them—without either disclosing the identities of their targets or downloading all call data in its entirety! In fact, protocols that make it possible to do this are well-known. This scenario is a special case of the secure two-party computation problem, in which two participants—here, a phone company A and a government agency B—cooperate in such a way that, on the one hand, B learns whatever he needs to about A's data, but, on the other hand, A has no idea what it was that B was interested in.

Secure two-party and multiparty computation, introduced by Andy Yao in 1982, is a fantastic tool that should be used here. After decades of theoretical research, 2008 saw it used in practice on a large scale for the first time: the Danish sugar-beet market participants used secure multiparty computation in order to agree on their pricing scheme. Previously, pricing sugar beets every year was a very challenging problem in Denmark because the participants did not trust each other with the information about what and how much they could produce or consume, but multiparty computation allowed them to calculate a price that was based on their private information, without revealing this information to each other.

Since 2008, more software tools that carry out secure two-party and multiparty computation have been developed, making it a practical reality. For example, a paper presented at the IEEE Symposium on Security and Privacy in 2014 ("Blind Seer: A Scalable Private DBMS" by Pappas et al.) presents a software system that the NSA could use right away, off the shelf, that would be a great improvement over just downloading and storing all the call records data. Instead, the Blind Seer system, a database server—administered, for example, by a phone company that cooperates with these efforts but is not trusted with the information about the government's targets—would store the data in an encrypted form. The NSA would be able to query the data and find the records it needs in almost the same way and with almost the same efficiency as with nonencrypted databases, and yet the database server would not learn anything about these queries or their results.

Exciting theoretical results abound too. For example, a paper published at Eurocrypt 2014 ("Fully Key-Homomorphic

Encryption, Arithmetic Circuit ABE and Compact Garbled Circuits" by Boneh et al.) shows that a secure solution in this context can, at least in principle, be extremely convenient: government agency B can just send to phone company A a piece of software that will repeatedly process A's call records and send B the results B needs (in encrypted form) such that A will not learn what it is that B is looking for, and B will not learn anything for which it does not have proper legal authority, such as a court order or warrant.

It was the U.S. government that funded the research described in both of these papers; more interestingly, it was funded *by our intelligence community*, through the Intelligence Advanced Research Projects Activity (IARPA) program. IARPA is part of the Office of the Director of National Intelligence—i.e., the office headed by James Clapper, a name now well-known to privacy activists and the public, and not in a positive way. It seems only fitting that our intelligence agencies should use it!

What has prevented these technological solutions from getting adopted? Perhaps cryptographers and policy makers are not speaking the same language. For example, I tried to explain how the NSA can use the Blind Seer system I discuss above to a policy maker. He raised an objection that is crucial if you are approaching the problem from the policy point of view but completely trivial if you are a computer scientist. He thought that the Blind Seer system might not work because their solution worked only for one phone company, and the NSA's system needs to look across different providers. To a computer scientist, it is clear that one simply needs to search, separately, for the relevant records among the data held by all the phone companies, but it's not necessarily clear to anyone else! It seems that policy makers working in this area would benefit from a crash course in computer science in general and cryptography in particular, while cryptographers would do well not only to create the most general solutions to these problems but also to work with specific examples that are of interest to our society.

Cryptography also gives us other tools for getting the best of both worlds: accountability for wrongdoers and yet privacy for everyone else. For example, anonymous credential systems allow users to prove that they are authorized to access a particular part of a system without revealing any other information about themselves, such as their names or any other persistent identifiers. Yet, it may be possible to identify users who go outside of their terms of service; for example, if a newspaper subscription authorizes a certain number of articles per day, it is possible to enforce that by making users who try to download more than that identifiable. Further, such systems can be extended with identity escrow that makes it possible to discover the user's identity in special circumstances, with the help of a trusted third party. Anonymous credentials have been extensively studied in the cryptographic literature and have been successfully used in test-case scenarios, such as in a course evaluation system at the University of Patras in Greece.

Cryptography also gives us tools to aggregate information for the purposes of scientific discovery, but in a way that respects the privacy of individuals who participate in such studies. The idea is to ensure that published data is *differentially private*, that is, even knowing everything about everyone in a particular study, it is hard to tell whether a particular individual has participated in the study or not—i.e., the difference an individual makes to a study is minuscule. It turns out that for many types of studies, it is possible to achieve differential privacy, and so we can benefit from the abundance of useful data out there and discover the underlying scientific truths—and yet not violate anyone's privacy in the process.

Thus, counterintuitively, cryptography gives us the tools to have our cake and eat it too. We can take advantage of the wealth of information out there in order to keep an eye out for criminals and terrorists, to conduct scientific studies, and to rule out unauthorized behavior. And yet, it can be done without violating the privacy of law-abiding individuals. To make it a reality, cryptographers and policy makers need to do a better job talking to each other.

COMING TO TERMS AND AVOIDING INFORMATION TECHNO-FALLACIES

Gary T. Marx

The editors of this volume asked contributors to write on "emerging challenges" to privacy and what can be done about them. Any child of the Enlightenment cannot but be inspired by the role that EPIC plays, the optimism that sustains it in the face of the new challenges technology brings, and the large megaphones possessed by its advocates. One must have a dream, and not to act in the face of abuse is to be a party to it. Yet as a contrarian mired in and slowed, but not stopped, by the complexity of well-intentioned pronouncements and policies, I find the frequent failure to be clearer about the meaning and connection of basic concepts and the failure to surface the tacit empirical and ethical assumptions on which positions are based troubling.

The specifics of surveillance, privacy, and information control of course change, but the fundamental questions and concepts endure, as do many techno-fallacies that undermine public policies appropriate for a democratic society. In a recently completed book (*Windows into the Soul: Surveillance and*

Gary T. Marx is professor emeritus at M.I.T.

Society in an Age of High Technology) and in articles at www
.garymarx.net, I identify basic concepts and a series of techno-
fallacies. Here, after a brief discussion of concepts, I turn to
some commonly held beliefs that I think are in error, or at least
unhelpful.

A conceptual map of new (and old) ways of collecting, analyzing, communicating, and using personal information is required, as is awareness of basic concepts and how they relate.
Explanation and evaluation require a common language for
the identification and measurement of surveillance's fundamental properties and settings. The richness of the empirical
must be disentangled and parsed into categories that can be
measured.

Surveillance practices need to be understood within specific
historical, cultural, institutional, and social structural settings
and the give-and-take of interaction. They require appreciation
(if not necessarily welcoming) of the ironies, paradoxes, trade-
offs, and value conflicts that limit the best-laid plans. Mush-
rooms do well in the dark, but so does injustice. Sunlight may
bring needed accountability through visibility, but it can also
blind and burn.

Privacy (whether as rules or as observable conditions about
the state of information apart from whether rules are present or
followed) and its cousin surveillance are neither good nor bad,
but *context* and *comportment* make them so. *Context* refers to
the type of institution or organization in question and to the
goals, rules, and expectations it is associated with. *Comportment* refers to the kind of behavior expected (whether based on
law or less formal cultural expectations) of, and actually shown
by, those in the various roles of agent, subject, third party, or

audience. While sharing some elements, differences in surveillance contexts involving coercion (government), care (parents and children), contracts (work), and free-floating accessible personal data (the personal and private within the public) need consideration. Surveillance is a generic process characteristic of living systems with information borders and not something restricted to spying or governments. Surveillance and privacy are not necessarily in opposition, and the latter can be a means of ensuring the former, as with access controls to information. While media attention to the problems associated with inappropriate surveillance (particularly by government) is present, there are also problems associated with the failure to use surveillance when it is appropriate.

The protection of information needs to be thought about within a framework broad enough to also include freedom of information. The common elements are rules about the protection and revelation of information. While these rules share elements, for policy purposes there are major differences between organizational secrecy and individual privacy, and the standards for the latter should not automatically be applied to the former. Traditional surveillance involving the senses is in some ways distinct from the new surveillance that involves technological enhancements of the senses.

Privacy, like surveillance, is a multidimensional concept whose contours are often ill defined, contested, negotiated, and fluid, dependent on the context and culture. Among the major forms are *informational, aesthetic, decisional,* and *proprietary* privacy. Physical or logistical protections for information or its revelation need to be considered apart from cultural ideas that support the protection or revelation of information. Privacy needs to be seen in its logical relationships to an extended family of terms such as *secrecy, confidentiality,* and *anonymity.* Both surveillance and communication can involve issues of privacy and autonomy. Surveillance can cross personal borders in order to take information, while communication can cross them in order to impart information. They may share issues of informed consent and respect for the dignity of the person and around the perception and meaning of the data or information involved. They can be temporally linked, as when surveillance serves as the means to direct communication (marketing based on purchases or life chances based on profiling).

The empirical claims and the value assumptions that nourish the optimistic techno-surveillance worldview found in the United States need to be better understood. Sometimes these form a relatively coherent and self-conscious ideology, or at least a perspective, as with governments, political parties, and interest groups such as the National Association of Manufacturers, the International Association of Chiefs of Police, and the National Association of Security Companies. More often, however, the beliefs can be found in dangling ad hoc snippets drawn on to justify an interest group's claims and actions.

In participating in the policy debate over the recent several decades I have often heard claims that, given my knowledge and values, sounded wrong, much as a musician hears notes as off-key. The off-key notes involve elements of substance as well as styles of mind and ways of reasoning. Sometimes these are direct; more often they are tacit—buried within seemingly commonsense, unremarkable (but unquestioned) assertions. The table below lists commonly encountered ideas that I think are often empirically, logically, or ethically unsupported.

INFORMATION AGE TECHNO-FALLACIES

A. Fallacies of Technological Determinism and Neutrality

1. The fallacy of autonomous technology and emanenative development and use
2. The fallacy of neutrality
3. The fallacy of quantification
4. The fallacy that the facts speak for themselves
5. The fallacy that technical developments must necessarily mean less privacy

B. Fallacies of Scientific and Technical Perfection

1. The fallacy of the 100 percent fail-safe system
2. The fallacy of the sure shot
3. The fallacy of delegating decision-making authority to the machine
4. The fallacy that technical solutions are to be preferred
5. The fallacy of the free lunch or painless dentistry
6. The fallacy that the means should determine the ends
7. The fallacy that technology will always remain the solution rather than become the problem

C. Fallacies Involving Subjects of Surveillance

1. The fallacy that individuals are best controlled through fear
2. The fallacy of a passive, nonreactive environment
3. The fallacy of implied consent and free choice
4. The fallacy that personal information is just another kind of property to be bought and sold
5. The fallacy that if critics question the means, they must necessarily be indifferent or opposed to the ends
6. The fallacy that only the guilty have to fear the development of intrusive technology (or if you've done nothing wrong, you have nothing to hide)

D. Fallacies of Questionable Legitimation

1. The fallacy of applying a war mentality to domestic surveillance
2. The fallacy of failing to value civil society

3. The fallacy of explicit agendas
4. The legalistic fallacy that just because you have a legal right to do something, it is the right thing to do
5. The fallacy of relativism or the least-bad alternative
6. The fallacy of single-value primacy
7. The fallacy of lowest-common-denominator morality
8. The fallacy that the experts (or their creations) always know what is best
9. The fallacy of the velvet glove
10. The fallacy that if it is new, it is better
11. The fallacy of equivalence or failing to note what is new
12. The fallacy that because privacy rights are historically recent and extend to only a fraction of the world's population, they can't be very important
13. The fallacy of legitimation via transference

E. Fallacies of Logical or Empirical Analysis

1. The fallacy of acontextuality
2. The fallacy of assumed representativeness
3. The fallacy of reductionism
4. The fallacy of a bygone golden age of privacy
5. The fallacy that correlation must equal causality
6. The fallacy of the short run
7. The fallacy that greater expenditures and more powerful and faster technology will continually yield benefits in a linear fashion
8. The fallacy that if some information is good, more is better
9. The fallacy of meeting rather than creating consumer needs
10. The fallacy of the double standard
11. The fallacy that because it is possible to successfully skate on thin ice, it is wise to do so
12. The fallacy of rearranging the deck chairs on the *Titanic* instead of looking for icebergs
13. The fallacy of confusing data with knowledge and technique with wisdom

The dominant surveillance discourse is not necessarily appreciably richer in fallacies than is the case for the claims of critics. However, it is *dominant*, and individuals clearly have socially patterned differential access to the ability to create and propagate surveillance and privacy worldviews. As such, it warrants greater attention.

Of course the views of all claimants must be examined, not only the advocates of technology. By adding "never" or otherwise reversing many of the techno-fallacies, we may see mirror-image fallacies held by some critics (e.g., the fallacy that technical solutions are never to be preferred). Other fallacies unique to critics may be noted. Thus some critics fail to appreciate the advantages of technology, the virtues of community, and the dangers of anarchy. A list of techno-fallacies for privacy advocates would include: the fallacy that with new technologies the sky is falling or the apocalypse approaching; that if you can imagine bad things happening, they surely will; that the people always know what's best (the populist fallacy); that privacy is an unlimited good (or if some privacy is good, more must be better); that privacy is primal (i.e., that it ought to take precedence over other values); that privacy is only an individual value rather than a social one; that privacy can only be taken from persons, rather than imposed upon them; that because something worked (or failed) in the past, it will in the future; that technology is always the problem and never the solution (the Luddite fallacy); and related to this, that technology can only be used to cross informational borders rather than to protect them.

In order to further constructive dialogue besides understanding any claimant's assumptions and possible fallacies, we need to know what rules the claimant plays by and what the game is. The worldview of those who start with advocacy rather than analysis is by definition self-serving. The rhetorical devices expected there differ from those of the academic analyst, who must start with questions, not answers, and question all claimants. The scholar of course serves his or her interests in the pursuit of truth. But especially because scholars are making truth claims, they must also strive for consistency and a strong tilt toward logic and evidence. In that regard several failings of academics can be noted: the overly broad academic generalization; the dressing of common sense (or nonsense) in multisyllabic jargon replete with esoteric references; the use of Ockham's razor to nitpickingly slice the world into too many categories; unduly timid waffling in the face of complexity and always-imperfect data; the failure to clearly enough differentiate value statements from scientific statements; and the reverse—failing to specify how the empirical within the value might be assessed. More a cheap shot than a fallacy is risk-free Monday-morning quarterbacking.

There is a path, however twisting, changing, and filled with brambles and illusions, between Tennyson's early-nineteenth-century optimism—"For I dipped into the future, far as the eye could see, saw the world, and all the wonders that would be"—and Einstein's twentieth-century worry that technological developments can become like an ax in the hands of a killer. That ambivalence is a hallmark of our age as we navigate between hope and dread and as unlevel playing fields are challenged and even change some, but still endure, and we continue to need protection both by and from authority. Yet there are strong grounds for keeping the faith with respect to both the importance of having a dream and the ameliorative potential of critical analysis. Ideas matter, as does political organizing.

While they (whether the state, commercial interests, or new, expanding public-private hybrid forms) are watching us, as scholars and citizens we need to watch them. Those committed to independent scholarship and the public good (however hard that can be to define), rather than to commercial interests or government contracts, have a vital role to play in publicizing what is happening or might happen, what happened in the past and happens elsewhere today, what is at stake and ways of thinking about this. Subjecting surveillance and privacy-hungry technologies to critical analysis and making them more visible and understandable hardly guarantees a just and accountable society, but it is surely a necessary condition for one.

WHEN SELF-HELP HELPS: USER ADOPTION OF PRIVACY TECHNOLOGIES

Aleecia M. McDonald

By the late 1990s, Privacy Enhancing Technologies (PETs) seemed like one answer to addressing user sovereignty online. If technology takes away privacy, the argument goes, surely it can also enable privacy. There are many barriers to users' adopting of PETs, including:

- Lack of obvious incentives to use PETs, stemming from, e.g.:
    a. A mistaken belief that strong laws protect online privacy
    b. A mistaken belief that companies would never collect the sort of data that forms the backbone of their business models
    c. Not realizing that invisible data collection goes on
- Lack of knowledge that privacy-enhancing tools exist
- Technically difficult installation procedures
- Terrible user experiences once tools are enabled

Due to press attention around Snowden's documents starting in June 2013, one might think incentives are now more

Aleecia M. McDonald is the director of privacy at Stanford's Center for Internet & Society.

obvious. If the first barrier is significant, we should expect to see a response from users. Indeed, a recent Harris poll found 47 percent of Americans changed their online activities as a result of NSA surveillance, with trust-based activities like online shopping highlighted. The Harris poll largely captured self-reported chilling effects. Does enhanced concern about privacy online also result in increased adoption of PETs? Signs point to yes.

DUCKDUCKGO

The privacy-protecting DuckDuckGo search engine does not suffer from all four barriers mentioned. The user experience is familiar rather than dire. DuckDuckGo does not require installation since users can access https://duckduckgo.com directly. Users may also configure DuckDuckGo as their default search engine with minimal work, eliminating the need to navigate specifically to the website. These characteristics are constant over time, allowing us to eliminate them as variables while contrasting DuckDuckGo use over the past four years. We are thus able to focus on the differences between lack of obvious incentive and lack of knowledge about DuckDuckGo, as seen in figure 1.

With all due caution that correlation is not causation, we see comparatively little increase in use after the installation of billboards advertising DuckDuckGo on California's Highway 101 and national news coverage about DuckDuckGo. These media events should start to address the knowledge barrier that DuckDuckGo exists but only has modest adoption gains. In contrast, we see major adoption after two events that highlight incentives to use DuckDuckGo, specifically Google's changes to their privacy policy (G) and initial publication of the Snowden documents (I). This suggests that removing overconfidence about online privacy is a major driver of PET use.

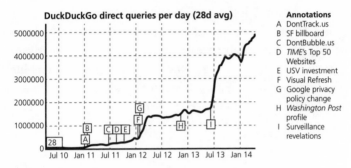

Figure 1: DuckDuckGo metrics are available from https://duckduckgo.com/traffic.html

While DuckDuckGo is an illustrative example to consider, the full story is not as simple as figure 1 suggests. Use skyrocketed when perceived incentives to use DuckDuckGo increased. However, the Snowden documents also resulted in more press about DuckDuckGo as an alternative search engine, as did Google's privacy policy changes. Both the knowledge barrier and the incentive barrier were intertwined and they changed together. Second, DuckDuckGo has agreements to ship as the default search engine for the Linux Mint distribution and two other open-source browsers, but those agreements are not annotated in figure 1. We do not know if they, or other similar agreements, changed adoption in any significant way. As real life is messy, there may be additional complications and interactions that we simply do not know about.

All caveats considered, it seems reasonable to form a working hypothesis that people will increase their use of PETs when they understand their privacy is at risk. This sounds obvious to the point of being trite, yet for decades we have been told that the absence of user action, including PET adoption, means users do not care about privacy. DuckDuckGo adoption patterns rather strongly refute such claims. It is not clear how those who believe the general absence of user action to protect privacy constitutes a "revealed preference" could explain the real-life results in shown in figure 1. It seems that users did not understand privacy risks, and once more users did understand, they took action to protect themselves.

TOR

Just as DuckDuckGo does not suffer from all of the typical barriers to PET use, by 2013 Tor was reasonably easy to install and use. Although improved, Tor remains slower than other browsers, which does impose a usability barrier.

Political unrest in Turkey provides a second natural experiment to examine. In the spring of 2014, the Turkish prime minister faced allegations of financial corruption. These allegations spread by Twitter and Facebook during the run-up to local elections that could have changed the majority party. The prime minister banned Twitter and Facebook, commenting that foreign software ought not be used to invade his privacy. An estimated eight people died during election-day protests. The courts reversed the Twitter ban days after the election. During the protests, information about PETs to improve personal privacy and circumvent the Twitter and Facebook bans spread more widely within the Turkish population. For example, pro-testers spray-painted Google's public DNS details on walls and circulated directions for Tor. As seen in figure 2, Tor use increased dramatically.

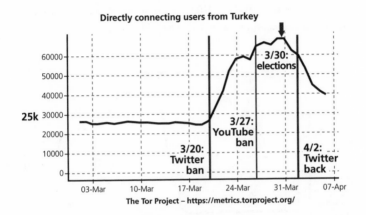

Figure 2: Annotated Tor use in Turkey showing an increase around elections

Once again, we see that a combination of obvious incentive and an increase in knowledge are combined in real life. Tor use more than doubled in the first week of the Twitter ban. In this case, however, it is not clear that privacy was the primary driver of Tor use. Free speech may well have been the key motivation, both in reading and writing messages around the elections. Tor use declined after elections even with the Twitter and YouTube bans still in place, suggesting communicating about the elections was at least one of the incentives for the increase in Tor use, not just being able to tweet socially without political purpose.

In August 2013, worldwide Tor use climbed due to what is

believed to be a botnet of infected PCs using Tor. We see no significant increase in worldwide Tor use immediately after the Snowden documents in June 2013, as shown in figure 3. By September, the increase in Tor use from the botnet completely swamps any effects we might have seen from Snowden. What we can say definitively is there is no sharp spike of Tor use in June and July as there was with DuckDuckGo.

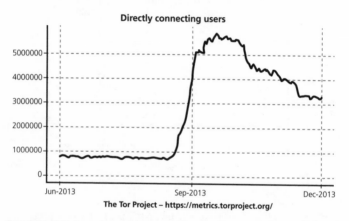

Figure 3: Worldwide Tor use increased due to botnets in August 2013

Even with the botnet skewing data, it appears there is no dramatic rise in Tor use between the press coverage of the Snowden documents in June and the botnet debut in August. Did Tor use initially stay stable because Tor was not specifically mentioned in early press coverage of NSA activities? Or was Tor so well-known before Snowden's documents that it was already used by anyone who cared to use it? Or perhaps people do not object to NSA data collection?

We cannot definitively answer these questions. However, given the DuckDuckGo data, it seems likely that world citizens are interested in privacy protections from the NSA. DuckDuckGo use spiked by July, but Tor use did not. Why did these two privacy tools follow different use patterns?

One possibility is that DuckDuckGo may have had more press coverage than Tor.[1] Using LexisNexis, in figure 4 we have the number of newspaper articles that mention both Tor and privacy, as well as the number of newspaper articles that mention both DuckDuckGo and privacy.

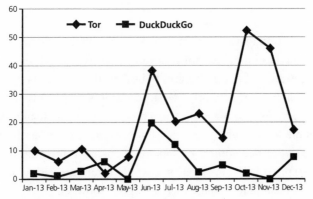

Figure 4: Number of news articles of "Tor AND privacy" and "DuckDuckGo AND privacy"

Both Tor and DuckDuckGo had few articles that mentioned them in the months prior to the Snowden documents. During the summer, both technologies had increased news coverage. Tor had more news mentions than DuckDuckGo, not fewer. Therefore the number of news articles cannot explain the difference in adoption.

Notice the large jump in news articles mentioning Tor in the fall, even greater than the jump in news articles around the Snowden documents. That increase is due to media coverage of the end of the Silk Road. In general, the type of news coverage that Tor and DuckDuckGo received was very different. For DuckDuckGo, a typical headline was something like, "Seven ways to keep your data safer." For Tor, headlines included weev, drug dealers, and Chinese hackers. DuckDuckGo is mentioned as something readers can use to protect themselves; Tor is more often than not described as something criminals use.

PGP

Pretty Good Privacy (PGP) is the poster child for studying barriers to adoption, spawning all too many security papers with the phrase "Why Johnny Can't" in the title. PGP adds an additional barrier: network effects. Just as it is no good to be the only person who owns a fax machine, going through all of the trouble to get public key encryption working is useless if you cannot persuade others to join you. Looking at the number of nonexpired PGP keys over time would be an interesting proxy to understand if PGP use increased post-Snowden.

Kristian Fiskerstrand runs SKS-keyservers.net and publishes basic metrics.[2] Figure 5 shows the increase in the number of OpenPGP keys over time. Notice the previously stable slope increases after June 2013.

As shown in figure 6, during the summer of 2013 the number of new keys created each day increased to three times what it had been prior to the release of the Snowden documents.

Nearly a year later, daily rates are still about twice as high as they had been prior to June.

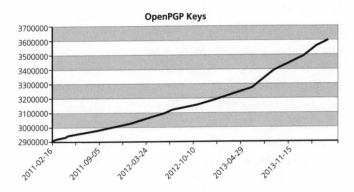

Figure 5: Cumulative number of OpenPGP keys over time

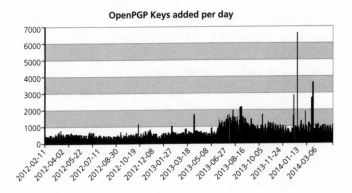

Figure 6: Number of new OpenPGP keys every day

OBSERVATIONS

DuckDuckGo and PGP show dramatic increases in use after June 2013, but Tor does not. Given how excruciatingly difficult PGP can be to install, particularly when contrasted to Tor and DuckDuckGo's relatively easy setup procedures, this suggests that traditional usability barriers are not the biggest hurdle to PET adoption. Rather, users' false sense of security online (including believing their privacy is protected by laws that do not exist in the United States) may be the biggest single barrier to taking steps to protect online privacy and security.

Tor did see strong user adoption in Turkey, which validates the idea that there is not some special nonobvious barrier to Tor use. It appears Tor lost a golden opportunity for increased worldwide adoption due to the way Tor is portrayed in the press. When Tor is seen as the tool of criminals, fewer people may want to try it out themselves, or even see any motivation to do so. This also suggests there is an opportunity for respected people to talk about using Tor. If we do not counter the impression that Tor belongs to the domain of rapscallions, that view may become a self-fulfilling conclusion.

In general, media coverage of the motivation to use a tool and the knowledge that the tool exists were intertwined in real life. An open question is how well ad campaigns for PETs would work, both with some sense of crisis and without.

Finally, even with all caveats about conclusions drawn from the messy conditions of real life, these case studies provide a reassertion that people care about privacy and are willing to take action when they know their privacy is at stake. Companies have claimed otherwise for years, even in the face of evidence to the contrary. Here is yet more evidence.

NOTES

1. Google Trends compares interest in news headlines containing "DuckDuckGo" or "Tor."
2. See https://sks-keyservers.net/status/key_development.php.

PROTECTING DATA PRIVACY IN EDUCATION

Dr. Pablo G. Molina

To become Homo sapiens—a "wise man"—one must learn. This is something that we do as human beings. We spend our lives learning. We may start with preschool singing and finish with watercolors or Spanish late in life. We may take guitar lessons or snowboarding classes. We may obtain a scuba diving certification, hone our sailing skills, or take a motorcycle safety course. It is because of this never-ending, lifelong quest to learn that many organizations accumulate vast amounts of information about our educational activities.

Some of us would like to save that information. Who was that great teacher in second-grade math? What courses did I take in my junior year in high school? How many classes did I skip in journalism school to play cards with friends instead? What was the worst grade that I ever received? Can I read again that assignment about Cervantes that I aced? Can I look at the embarrassing image that I submitted for my photography final? I want access to that information.

Dr. Pablo G. Molina is the chief information officer at the American Association of Law Schools and at Southern Connecticut State University.

I am sorry that some of this information is lost due to my poor memory, and to my even poorer preservation skills—to say nothing of the lassitude of the administrators who ran my old school. Today, however, losing that information is the only way to ensure that no unauthorized people will access it. I want to control access by others to my educational information. I want my daughter to know that I was a straight-A student; at the same time, I do not want my graduate students to know about my school suspension in the eighth grade. I wanted the admissions committee of my doctoral program to have access to my Graduate Record Examination score; however, I do not want employers to examine those scores and to draw conclusions about my professional abilities.

Many parties want information about our educational struggles for a variety of reasons, including efficiency improvements and marketing. How many students who took remedial math failed to graduate from college in four years? From how many courses or programs were students denied admission because of limited supply and excess demand? What was the average grade in introductory statistics in our undergraduate psychology program? How long did test takers hesitate before answering certain multiple-choice questions on the privacy professional certification exam? How do we mine our historic educational databases to target Connecticut residents for the Go Back to Get Ahead college completion program?

Regardless of the reasons for hoarding data, amassing this information exposes all learners to two major risks: data breaches and organizational abuses. Data breaches are unintended disclosures of educational data. Organizational abuses happen when organizations exploit accumulated data, the by-product of educational activities, beyond the expectations of the data subjects, often without their knowledge.

Georgetown University suffered or caused three major data breaches when it accidentally exposed the privately identifiable information of many of its constituents. In 2008, 38,000 Social Security numbers leaked from the university when someone stole an external, unencrypted hard disk drive from an office. On another occasion, a researcher failed to enable the necessary information security controls to protect a database server, which was then compromised by hackers. In a separate incident, a university technology professional stored unsecured confidential information on a mobile device and lost it.

Georgetown University was not alone. Team Shatter Inc., an information technology company, created a parody of the March Madness college basketball competition in the United States. They paired colleges and universities suffering embarrassing data losses against each other, until one of them earned the dubious honor of becoming the Higher Education Data Breach Madness "champion." In 2011, Virginia Commonwealth University won after reporting a data breach of 176,567 records. Incompetent administrators in educational institutions and incompetent executives in the corporations that provide services for those educational institutions expose student data to unauthorized users.

There are numerous examples of organizational abuses. One of the most prominent cases of an organizational abuse was that of inBloom in 2014. The mission of this nonprofit was to serve as a secure repository of public student data and to share that data with some of the technology vendors supporting the schools. The questionable privacy practices of inBloom led to its demise, as state and district partners abandoned the initiative, in spite of the $100 million financial backing of the Bill and Melinda Gates Foundation and the Carnegie Corporation of New York.

Three major actors are responsible for these data leaks and organizational abuses: academic administrators, educational entrepreneurs, and hackers. To ensure the privacy of educational information, we must influence the behavior of these three agents. We need better laws, better technologies, and better advocacy.

We need better laws. Policies without teeth—that is, without real penalties for misbehavior—have little effect. With the existing legal framework, neither academic administrators nor educational entrepreneurs have compelling reasons to invest in the custody of student data. Who owns the information? Does it belong to the learners, the educators, the entrepreneurs, or the government agencies overseeing education? Like medical information, educational information belongs, first and foremost, to the learners themselves. As such, they have the right to opt in or out of data collection, to control the collection of data, to decide who has access to it for what reasons, and to have it corrected or expunged upon request.

These are not novel principles or new ideas. These principles were enshrined in the United States as the Fair Information Practice Principles in 1973 and encoded in the U.S. Privacy Act of 1974. They substantially influenced the enactment of FERPA, the Family Educational Rights and Privacy Act, in 1974 and many of its amendments. In theory, FERPA protects student information over its life cycle, from kindergarten through graduate school. But the truth of the matter is that FERPA violations are not privately enforceable and the Department of Education has yet to execute its nuclear option—withdrawal of all federal funding to an offending school—for the most egregious FERPA violations. FERPA applies to all schools that receive funds under an applicable program of the U.S. Department of Education. What about vocational schools, distance-learning websites, and foreign-based education outfits? In the United States, these organizations do not have to comply with any privacy laws. Only the Federal Trade Commission could investigate their privacy abuses as consumer protection issues.

With other activists on my side, I argue that the Department of Education should issue a Bill of Rights for students of all ages to serve as a framework to guide student data privacy practices in primary, secondary, and tertiary education. Most importantly, we hope for a framework that will shape educational practices comprehensively, including vocational education and unregulated sectors of the education market, in the United States and abroad, online and in real life.

We need better technologies. Without technology platforms, processes, and people designed for privacy and information security, we cannot ensure that educational administrators will exercise due custody of their data. Why can't we do this in education? What is so fundamentally different about education that we think that the protection of learners' data is less important than the protection of financial, medical, or electoral information?

Some argue that academic information is a low priority for hackers worldwide. This is not necessarily true, as many primary, secondary, tertiary, and vocational academic institutions worldwide have experienced firsthand. Hacking, like other crimes, is a question of motive, means, and opportunity. The motive is clear. Academic records can be exploited for a variety of hostile purposes, including the public embarrassment and even extortion of its targets by private individuals, yellow journalists, or political enemies. They provide useful ammunition to attack business competitors. They can be used to disqualify rival classmates competing for employment. According to the Verizon 2014 Data Breach Investigations Report, the educational sector is one of the top targets under cyber attack.

We need better advocacy. We need the unwavering commitment of civil society organizations like Sheila Kaplan's National Opt-Out Campaign and the Electronic Privacy Information Center's litigation activity. The value of their work becomes apparent when reading Marc Rotenberg and Khaliah Barnes's "Amassing Student Data and Dissipating Privacy Rights" piece, published in 2013. We also need the thoughtful thinking of academics like Fordham Law professor Joel Reidenberg. These activists and others like them shed light on the risks of insufficiently protecting educational data. They educate legislators, government officers, educational administrators, and entrepreneurs on the importance of and value of protecting student privacy.

So what? What is the big deal? Who could be hurt if we do nothing? Among the vulnerable are students with disabilities or special needs, who would like to control the disclosure of this information. While it may be relevant and useful for a law student to disclose that he or she has attention deficit disorder, such a disclosure may be altogether irrelevant in a distance-learning security certification course. Students who need to take remedial courses in math or English may also want to choose who knows about this over time. Nondegree students, including life learners, who harbor multidisciplinary interests and curiosities and who experiment with different courses may want to keep some of their educational experiences confidential. This would include the millions of people worldwide who have attended any MOOCs, Massive Online Open Courses. In general, anybody who ever signed up for a controversial course, submitted a controversial assignment, or had a less-than-perfect academic record could be at risk.

Like many, I signed up for MOOCs from institutions like Yale University or the University of Washington. I was unable to finish the courses. My interest waned over time, to the point that I did not do the assignments or stopped participating in the online discussions. I dropped out of the courses without so much as notifying the organizations that ran them, e.g., Coursera or EdX, that I had done so. My disclosure here aside, I would not want my employer to know that I am a MOOC dropout. Similarly, I would not want anybody to know that I was expelled from Northern Virginia Community College, where I unsuccessfully signed up for a motorcycle safety class, twice.

Educational entrepreneur and Knewton founder and CEO Jose Ferreira said it best in his blog in 2013. "Big data in education is a hot topic, and getting hotter. Proponents tout its potential for reform. Detractors raise privacy concerns. Skeptics don't see the point of it all." Edupreneurs like Ferreira would like to collect every piece of data that they can collect because it adds value to their companies and opens new business opportunities. While some of the entrepreneurs extol the virtues of privacy and self-regulation, the truth is that unregulated businesses may all too easily err on the side of earnings rather than on the side of student privacy.

The risks, if we do nothing, are bigger than we think. What happens in education in the United States affects other countries. Often, USAID funds shape educational policy in recipient countries. Educational entrepreneurs and academic consultants steer educational systems abroad toward standardized tests, massive data collection and mining, technology adoption, partnerships with the private sector, etc. Without adequate privacy protections, the United States may export its privacy risks for educational data to other jurisdictions.

HOW MIGHT SYSTEM AND NETWORK SECURITY INTERACT WITH PRIVACY?

Peter G. Neumann

This article considers some of the technological potentials of what the security of computer systems and networks might contribute to privacy, as well as some of the inherent limitations. Ideally, security and privacy should be synergistic, rather than conflicting. However, at present we are facing a world in which almost everything we depend upon technologically is typically riddled with vulnerabilities whose accidental triggering or intentional exploitation could compromise security, and thus could further exacerbate the extent and likelihood of privacy violations. Ideally, what we need are inherently trustworthy systems and networks and user and administrator and operational procedures, where trustworthiness encompasses a range of critical requirements such as information and system security, integrity, reliability, interoperability, availability, and survivability in the presence of adversaries, and so on. Unfortunately, the current state of the art in technological and administrative trustworthiness is truly abysmal, compared with what is needed. As a result, the reality is that we have neither adequate security nor adequate privacy.

Computer-communication technology has evolved over the years, with many would-be improvements in hardware

---

Peter G. Neumann has been in SRI's Computer Science Lab since September 1971, and is now its Senior Principal Scientist.

and software techniques for user authentication, access controls, system integrity, cryptographically based applications, firewalls, robust networks, cloud servers, pervasive monitoring, misuse-detection systems, and so on. In addition, numerous operational procedures, administrative guidelines, and legal measures have attempted to support technological security measures. All of these approaches have the potential in different ways to help enhance privacy. However, thus far these approaches have been seriously inadequate.

On the other hand, even with any hoped-for dramatic improvements in system and network security, there are some severe limitations to what combinations of such technological factors might hope to achieve, even when combined with procedural controls and enforcement of sensible legislation. In particular, many of our privacy problems are extrinsic to the computer-communication information technologies—in the sense that they are beyond the purview of systemic controls. Thus, the real nature of our privacy difficulties represents a total-system problem that encompasses a combination of the intrinsic weaknesses of our computer-based technology and the extrinsic nature of many privacy concerns.

Many people have asserted that the best is the enemy of the good, resulting in lowest common denominators. Realistically, that which is often considered *good* is simply *not good enough*—especially for critical or sensitive applications.[1] Because there can never be perfectly secure systems (especially when having to confront ubiquitous penetrations, denial-of-service attacks, and insider misuse), some of the extrinsic problems are likely to persist despite many of the would-be systemic and procedural measures.

Sadly, despite some local improvements, the trustworthiness of our systems does not seem to have increased sufficiently in the past few decades. As a result, the problems of privacy have only gotten worse. For example, compare the world today with the state of the art in 1995.[2] We see immediately that many of the types of problems described in *Computer-Related Risks* are still recurring regularly today, and many of the remedies suggested there and elsewhere in the past (e.g., in reports of the National Research Council[3]) have not been adopted. Furthermore, the privacy problems are escalating in scale, in scope, and in magnitude of risks, inconvenience, and fraud.

With respect to privacy, the simplistic practice of storing sensitive information in insecure systems connected to the Internet or otherwise accessible (e.g., by phone lines or wirelessly) is not very wise, but of course is standard practice. Trusting such information to networked cloud servers administered by potentially untrustworthy third parties is even less sensible from security and privacy perspectives, although it may be very advantageous financially. A simplistic summary of the situation is that once information leaves the purview of locally administered computer systems, almost all bets are off. To mix a few metaphors, when Pandora's cat is out of the barn, the genie won't go back in the closet.

The ultimate question here seems to be this: whom and what do you have to trust, especially if the systems and operators are not all trustworthy, and when faced with malevolent insiders and outsiders who effectively can become insiders? Although it is generally possible to design and implement systems and networks that are more resilient in the face of erroneous human behavior, it is much more difficult to have comparable approaches that provide adequate security in the face of serious attempts at misuse. This statement becomes even more complicated when attacks are coordinated, distributed, and widespread. However, even efforts that are focused on specific individuals rather than broad-brush compromises of many individuals can have devastating effects.

Some technological relief might be anticipated. For example, we could rely on a system currently being developed for the Defense Advanced Research Projects Agency (DARPA) in joint ongoing work involving SRI International and the University of Cambridge. Our newly designed hardware[4] enforces trustworthy sandboxing of suspicious code with arbitrarily fine-grained access controls—which together can greatly restrict adverse behavior. The hardware design runs on two different field-programmable gate array platforms, with a newly designed capability-based coprocessor running alongside a MIPS64 implementation. It is also formally based, including the hardware specification language, the inclusion of the full suite of SRI formal analysis tools into the compiler that builds an efficient FPGA image from the high-level specifications, and the potential for formally analyzing some of the low-level software as well. The hardware supports FreeBSD applications. The hardware and software are available under open-source licenses. With formal methods built into the hardware build chain, this system has the potential to significantly advance the enforcement of finer-grained security policies. In addition, this effort includes TESLA, a newly developed facility that permits dynamic detection of real-time events that are never supposed to happen.[5]

One reason I introduce the previous paragraph here is to

be able to specifically motivate the following question: even if we were to use such a demonstrably trustworthy hardware-software platform, how might this diminish the privacy problems? Several positive factors stand out. For example, suppose we had system and network architectures that employ sandbox-like compartmentalization and fine-grained access controls, coupled with cryptographically based user and intersystem authentication (i.e., eschewing fixed passwords) and sensible policies for computer security and privacy, along with pervasive monitoring of certain potentially damaging user activities. Such a holistic constructive approach could considerably diminish the opportunities for undesirable data exfiltration that would remain undetected. That would be a very encouraging start.

In summary, in the ever-escalating struggles between defense and offense, privacy violations also seem to be escalating in scale and frequency in recent years. To reverse this trend, it is clearly essential that the architectural and implementation trustworthiness of our baseline computer systems and networks must increase substantially. However, even if that were the case, and even if the technology were invoked pervasively and applied wisely to its fullest potential in operational practice (which itself might seem to be a pipe dream), some significant privacy risks would always remain—especially those that are extrinsic. Also, human misjudgments and errors of commission or omission would still be likely, although extrinsic misuse might even be reduced somewhat overall. However, misuse by knowledgeable insiders—and especially overly omnipotent system administrators—would always remain a risk. Thus, we need a holistic approach that encompasses dramatic technological improvements, procedural efforts that are more than palliative best practices, legislation (be careful what you ask for—you may get something worse), enforcement, and common sense. As usual, there are no easy answers.

NOTES

1. Peter G. Neumann, "The Foresight Saga, Redux: Short-Term Thinking Is the Enemy of the Long-Term Future," *Communications of the ACM* 55, no. 10 (October 2012), http://www.csl.sri .com/neumann/cacm228.pdf.

2. Peter G. Neumann, *Computer-Related Risks* (Reading, MA: Addison-Wesley, 1995).

3. D.D. Clark et al., *Computers at Risk: Safe Computing in the Information Age* (Washington, DC: National Academy Press, 1990); F.B. Schneider, ed., *Trust in Cyberspace* (Washington, DC: National Academy Press, 1998).

4. Jonathan Woodruff, Robert N.M. Watson, David Chisnall, et al., "The CHERI Capability Model: Revisiting RISC in an Age of Risk," *Proceedings of the Forty-First International Symposium on Computer Architecture* (Minneapolis, MN: ISCA, 2014), https:// www.cl.cam.ac.uk/research/security/ctsrd/pdfs/201406-isca2014 -cheri.pdf.

5. Jonathan Anderson, Robert N.M. Watson, David Chisnall, et al., "TESLA: Temporally Enhanced System Logic Assertions," *Proceedings of the 2014 European Conference on Computer Systems* (Amsterdam: EuroSys, 2014), https://www.cl.cam.ac.uk/research /security/ctsrd/pdfs/201404-eurosys2014-tesla.pdf.

"RESPECT FOR CONTEXT": FULFILLING THE PROMISE OF THE WHITE HOUSE REPORT[1]

Helen Nissenbaum

In February 2012, the Obama White House unveiled the Consumer Privacy Bill of Rights (2012, 9) embedded in a comprehensive report, "Consumer Data Privacy in a Networked World: A Framework for Protecting Privacy and Promoting Innovation in the Global Digital Economy." The report and bill of rights, which signaled direct White House interest in privacy and buoyed hopes that change might be in the air, were cautiously endorsed by a range of parties—public interest advocates, industry leaders and associations, and government agencies—who have disagreed with one another on virtually everything else to do with privacy.[2]

Of the seven principles proposed in the Consumer Privacy Bill of Rights, six are recognizable as kin of traditional fair information practices, embodied, for example, in the OECD Privacy Guidelines. The third principle of "Respect for Context" (PRC), the expectation that "companies will collect, use, and

Helen Nissenbaum is professor of media, culture and communication, and Computer Science, at New York University, where she is also Director of the Information Law Institute.

disclose personal data in ways that are consistent with the context in which consumers provide the data" (p. 47), is intriguingly novel. *Context*, however, is a mercilessly ambiguous term with potential to be all things to all people. Its meanings range from the colloquial and general to the theorized and specific and shades in between. If determining the meaning of *context* were not challenging enough, determining what it means to respect it opens further avenues of ambiguity.

From a virtually endless set of possibilities, four interpretations are particularly interesting: context as technology platform or system, context as business model or practice, context as industry or sector, and context as social domain. Which one is the right one is the question I address in this essay. As I argue below, whether the Privacy Bill of Rights fulfills its promise as a watershed for privacy, whether the principle of respect for context is an active ingredient in the momentum will depend on which one of these interpretations drives public and private regulation going forward.

Although other interpretations have appeared in connection with privacy, I focus on these four because they imply divergent policy directions and also because they reflect persistent voices in discussions leading up to and following the White House report.

Context as Technology: In more than one hundred years of worrying about privacy, technological development has been a major impetus for societal attention. The contemporary moment is a case in point with a focus on the realm of information and digital networks—the Internet, and the myriad platforms and systems sitting atop (or below) it, such as mobile devices, e-mail, social networks, cloud service, and the Web itself. Most of us readily talk of communication and transaction taking place *online* or *in* cyberspace and see associated privacy problems as distinctive to these electronically mediated contexts. It is a short distance to conceive of this technological substrate and its social networks, Twitter, Wikipedia, mobile apps, and location-based services as a context. In such instances material properties of respective media, systems, or platforms shape—moderate, magnify, enable—the activities, transactions, and interactions that they mediate, as well as the ways information is tracked, gathered, analyzed, and disseminated. *Respect* for contexts, under this interpretation, would require policies to be heedful of systems' and platforms' natural function.

Context as Business Model or Practice: According to this interpretation, it is not technology per se that defines privacy rules of the road but distinctive business models and practices. Interpreted as the model or practice of a particular business, context is shaped by the nature and aims of that business and the practices it pursues in order to achieve these aims. This is an interpretation supported in the comments of many incumbents in the IT and information industries. Taking Web search as an example, whereas the underlying technological system may accumulate search logs containing information about personally identifiable individuals, the business model may define how long the logs are kept, how they are used, and with whom they are shared.

Context as Industry or Sector: Adopting the interpretation of context as sector or industry broadens the unit of analysis from individual businesses to the sector of industry in which they function. It also is compatible with the prevailing sectoral policy environment in the United States, which largely has regulated privacy protection on a sector-by-sector basis. By merging sector and industry I am not suggesting their meanings are identical but acknowledging that those who favor this interpretation have used these terms interchangeably in their comments. According to this interpretation, respect for context would amount to adherence to the set of rules or norms developed by, for, and within respective sectors or industries.

Context as Social Domain: This interpretation, supported by the theory of contextual integrity, presents contexts as social spheres, constituents of the differentiated social space of everyday life, including instances such as education, health care, politics, commerce, religion, family and home life, recreation, marketplace, and work. Spheres generally comprise characteristic activities and practices, functions (or roles), aims, purposes, institutional structure, values, and action-governing norms. Norms governing the flow of information form a subclass of these norms; context-specific informational norms (from here on, "informational norms") are crucial to contextual integrity. To flesh out what it would mean to respect context as social sphere requires a brief detour through the theory of contextual integrity.

Where other accounts of privacy focus on exposure of personal information or loss of control by data subjects, the theory of contextual integrity cites appropriateness of flow, namely those data flows that comport with legitimate informational norms, as a fundamental tenet. Whether a particular flow, or transmission of information from one party to another, is appropriate depends on the type of information in question, about whom it is, by whom and to whom it is transmitted, and the conditions or constraints under which this transmission takes place. According to contextual integrity's model of information flow the critical parameters are identified as: *Actors*—subject, sender, recipient—ranging over context-relevant functions, or roles, or acting in capacities associated with respective contexts. These functional roles include the familiar—physician, nurse, patient, teacher, senator, voter, polling station volunteer, mother, friend, uncle, priest, merchant, customer, congregant, policeman, judge, and, of course, many more. The parameter of *information type*, likewise, ranges over variables derived from the ontologies of specific domains. In health care, these could include symptomologies, medical diagnoses, diseases, pharmacological drugs; in education, they may include cognitive aptitude, performance measures, learning outcomes; in politics, party affiliations, votes cast, donations; and so forth. *Transmission principle*, the third parameter, designates the terms, or constraints, under which information flows. Think of it as a sluice gate. Abstractly conceived, the transmission principle has not been explicated in scholarly or policy discussions even though, in practice, its role in social convention, regulation, and law is pivotal. Control over information by the information subject can, in its terms, be understood as but one (albeit an important one) among an extensive range of options, including "in confidence," "with third-party authorization," "as required by law," "bought," "sold," "reciprocal," and "authenticated."

It bears emphasizing that the three parameters—actors, information type, and transmission principles—are independent. None can be reduced to the other two, nor can any one of them carry the full burden of defining privacy expectations. This is why past efforts to reduce privacy to a particular class of information (say, "sensitive" information) or to one transmission principle (say, control over information) were doomed to fail. For decades, these reductive efforts, in my view, have invited ambiguity and confusion in our understanding of privacy and have hindered progress in attempts to regulate its protection. Control over information may be an important transmission principle, but always with respect to particular actors and particular information types, all specified against the backdrop of a particular social context.[3]

Contextual integrity is achieved when actions and practices comport with informational norms. It is violated when actions or practices defy expectations by disrupting entrenched or normative information flows. Because informational norms model privacy expectations, it is no surprise when people react with annoyance, indignation, and protest when contextual integrity has been violated. Contextual integrity thus offers a diagnostic tool with prima facie explanatory and predictive capacities, providing a more highly calibrated view of factors relevant to privacy than traditional dichotomies such as disclose/not disclose, private/public.

Diagnosing a disruption in entrenched flow is but a start; being able to *evaluate* it is crucial to the moral sway of contextual integrity. Disruptive technologies, such as enhanced health indicators; new forms of communication and association, such as through social networks; and information search tools online offer great value. How to distinguish positive opportunities from those that violate privacy is an important challenge. To meet it, contextual integrity calls for a comparative assessment of preexisting flow against novel flow involving three layers of analysis: One considers the interests of key affected parties—the benefits they enjoy, the costs and risks they suffer. This largely economic approach, which dominates the policy arena in standard stakeholder analyses, offers only a partial view of what is at stake. A second layer considers general moral and political values. Thus, beyond straightforward trade-offs that might optimize overall benefit, this layer enjoins us to consider whether costs and benefits are justly distributed. Other core values identified in the privacy literature are democracy, unfair discrimination, informational harm, equal treatment, autonomy, identity formation, and a range of civil liberties.[4] Finally, we must consider context-specific values, ends, and purposes. These may help resolve conflicts that have long stumped us, such as privacy versus security, privacy versus profit, and so forth. A contextual analysis may reveal that freedom should trump in a given context, say a library, while security in another, say an airport. Contextual integrity offers a thoughtful way beyond the banal dichotomies of privacy versus business interests, versus national security, public safety, and freedom of expression. This layer insists that privacy, as appropriate information flows, serves not merely the interests of individual information subjects, but also contextual, social ends and values.

According to this account of context as social domain, *respect for context* is respect for contextual integrity.

To see why this account is the only one of the four with the potential to bring about significant advancement in protecting privacy, we take a closer look at the White House Privacy Bill of Rights. The debt to traditional "Fair Information Practices" (FIPs) is clear with principles of transparency, security, access and accuracy, and accountability, which line up with equivalent FIPs; respect for context, however, is not linked with any single principle but associated jointly with two equivalents: purpose specification ("The purposes for which personal data are collected should be specified no later than at the time of data collection and the subsequent use limited to the fulfillment of those purposes or such others as are not incompatible with these purposes and as are specified on each occasion of change of purpose" [p. 58]) and use limitation ("Personal data should not be disclosed, made available or otherwise used for purposes other than those specified . . . except . . . (a) with the consent of the data subject; or (b) by the authority of law" [p. 58]).

But purposes are not given in the principles themselves, resulting in a code that is either admirably adaptable or substantively empty. Purpose specification is the wild card, potentially creating a Trojan horse out of use limitation, collection limitation (often called data minimization), and even security and data quality. Unless and until purposes are shaped by substantive requirements, FIPs constitute a mere shell, formally defining relationships among the principles and laying out procedural steps to guide information flows.[5]

Whether the Consumer Privacy Bill of Rights devolves to this procedural formulation of FIPs or fulfills its promise of positive change depends on how we interpret context. I have argued that context understood as social domain is the most viable basis for progress among the four alternatives we have considered.

Under the interpretation of context as business model or practice, context would be determined by the exigencies of a particular business and ensuing policies, presumably communicated via terms of service. For online commerce, a merchant may reasonably require a consumer's address and valid payment information, but if business purpose is a blank check and political economy is all that shapes the relationship between the information collector and information subject, there is no recourse to standards beyond business expedience. By definition, each business entity determines what is and is not expedient. This may mean buying and selling information resources, extracting information resources from transactions, and using information with no restriction (except in the few sectors covered by privacy legislation). Even admitting the importance of business to society, its parochial needs are not sound footing for privacy's moral imperative.

What about context as technology platform or system? It is quite sensible to refer to a Facebook profile, a Bing search, a Fitbit group, the Web, and an e-mail exchange as contexts, but a mistake if respect for context is a bellwether for privacy. Letting technological affordance define moral imperative would mean that platform or system not only determines what information flows *can* happen but what flows *ought* to happen. Doubtless technologies shape contexts, may even constitute them. They alter practice and sometimes pull norms and standards along with them. New technologies may reconfigure ontologies, yield new categories of information, new types of actors and modes of dissemination. These may rightly call for a review of entrenched norms and spur new norms where none previously existed. But allowing these systems fully to account for the meaning of respect for context allows material design to define ethical and political precepts. It leads to distortions in regulation, responsive to details of technology outside its social significance. This places these systems beyond the pale of normative judgment, but where respect for context is a bellwether for privacy, it is a mistake to confuse technological contexts with those that define legitimate privacy expectations.

Interpreting context as sector or industry, which aligns well with the U.S. sectoral approach to privacy regulation, overcomes some of the drawbacks of context as business model because, instead of devolving to policies serving the interests of individual businesses, norms of information flow would be guided by a collective mission—ideally, collective best practice. Including sectors beyond industry and business, such as education, health care, politics, family, or religion, could extend the range of *appropriate* informational rules beyond serving parochial interests of business incumbents. Yet, ironically, as the scope of sectors is broadened, their conception edges in the direction of social spheres around which the theory of contextual integrity is oriented.

Interpreted as respect for contextual integrity, the principle of respect for context would require information flows to be characterized in terms of information types, actors, and transmission principles and evaluated in terms of the balance of interests and impacts on values and contextual aims. Such evaluations extend beyond conventional stakeholder interests and even beyond the general moral and political values widely acknowledged in privacy discussions. Context is not only a passive backdrop against which the interests of affected parties are measured, balanced, and traded off. In addition, context defines *how* these interests and values should be weighed. The integrity of contexts *themselves* is a final arbiter of information practices—vibrant marketplace, effective health care, sound education, truly democratic governance, and strong, trusting families and friendships.

In sum, for the Consumer Privacy Bill of Rights to advance privacy protection beyond its present state, much hangs on how context, in the principle of respect for context, is understood. Four contenders jockey for preeminence: business model, technology, sector, and social domain. I have argued that the fourth holds the greatest potential. Respecting context as *business model* offers no prospect of advancement beyond the present state of affairs. Respecting context as *sector* (or industry) fares somewhat better, though how much better this approach meaningfully advances privacy protection depends on how sectors are defined. The problem is particularly acute for the "information sector," where the proverbial fox would be guarding the henhouse. Further, if industrial sectors dominate the way sectors are conceived, the influence of sectors such as health care, education, religion, and politics will be diminished, or the commercial aspects of these industries may play a disproportionate role. A purely technological understanding of context would mean technical affordances and constraints would define legitimate expectations of privacy. But so doing gets things exactly backward, draining respect for context of moral clout. Our morally legitimate expectations, shaped by context and other factors, should drive design and define the responsibilities of developers, not the other way around.

According to the interpretation of context as *social domain*, respecting context means respecting informational norms that promote general ethical and political values, as well as context-specific ends, purposes, and values. Informational norms must specify all relevant parameters—actors (functioning in roles), information types, and transmission principles—or yield rules that are partial and ambiguous. In revealing critical dependencies between social values and appropriate information flows, contextual integrity once and for all debunks the fallacy of privacy as valuable for individuals alone.

Contexts are shaped by technology, business practice, and industry sector. They may also be constituted by geographic location, relationship, agreement, culture, religion, and era, and much more. In individual cases, any of these factors could qualify and shape peoples' expectations of how information about us is gathered, used, and disseminated. No one of them, however, provides the right level of analysis or carries the same moral and political weight as social domain. Accordingly, I offer an amendment to the Consumer Privacy Bill of Rights's principle of respect for context:

Respect for context means consumers have a right to expect that companies will collect, use, and disclose personal data in ways that are consistent with the [social] context in which consumers provide the data.

NOTES

1. This essay is drawn from a longer article greatly indebted to Solon Barocas, Emily Goldsher-Diamond, Mike Hinze, Chris Hoofnagle, and James Rule. The project was supported by NSF CNS-1355398 and DGE-0966187 and the Intel Science and Technology Center for Social Computing.
2. See M. Hoffman, "Obama Administration Unveils Promising Consumer Privacy Plan, but the Devil Will Be in the Details," Electronic Frontier Foundation, 2012; D. Hoffman, "White House Releases

Framework for Protecting Privacy in a Networked World," *Policy@ Intel* blog, February 23, 2012; "White House Unveils Consumer Privacy Bill of Rights," *EPIC Alert,* 19.04, February 29, 2012; and C. Civil, "President Obama's Privacy Bill of Rights: Encouraging a Collaborative Process for Digital Privacy Reform," *Berkeley Technology Law Journal,* March 12, 2012.

3. See H. Nissenbaum, *Privacy in Context: Technology, Policy and the Integrity of Social Life* (Stanford, CA: Stanford Law, 2010) for a full account.

4. See Nissenbaum, *Privacy in Context,* especially part 2.

5. Ibid.

PRIVACY, AUTONOMY, AND INTERNET PLATFORMS

Frank Pasquale

W hen do Internet platforms start stunting users, rather than enabling them to become what they want to be? Facebook's recent psychology experiment sharply poses that question for those on both sides of the platform.[1] Ordinary Facebookers, resigned to endure ever more intrusive marketing manipulation, were thrown for a loop by the news that they may be manipulated for no commercial reason at all. Researchers inside Facebook (and their university collaborators) saw their own identity questioned. Were they true scientists or some new kind of inquirer?

It's time to deepen the story of the experiment as a "loss of autonomy," by connecting the strictures imposed on insiders and outsiders. Ordinary users can't access, challenge, or try to adapt the code that Facebook uses to order their news feeds, except in the crude and stylized ways offered by the company. Social scientists have to play by Facebook's rules to get access to the data they need—and we can probably assume that a more informed consent process was either tacitly or explicitly rejected as too much of an interference with the ordinary business of

Frank Pasquale has taught information and health law at Seton Hall since 2004.

Facebooking. So the restricted autonomy of the researchers in turn led to the impairment of the autonomy of the users. This exemplar of values sacrificed in the name of market rationality is a microcosm of much larger trends in ordinary users' experience of the Web, and researchers' experience of their own craft.

ALL TO IMPROVE USER EXPERIENCE

Ask an Internet platform spokesperson why his or her firm made nearly any decision, and you'll hear some variation on "to improve user experience." But we all know that it's only a certain kind of user experience that is really valued and promoted. For Facebook to continue to meet Wall Street's demands for growth, its user base must grow and/or individual users must become more "productive." Predictive analytics demands standardization: forecastable estimates of revenue per user. The more a person clicks on ads and buys products, the better. Secondarily, the more a person draws other potential ad clickers in—via clicked-on content, catalyzing discussions, crying for help, whatever—the more valuable they become to the platform. The "model users" gain visibility, subtly instructing by example how to act on the network. They'll probably never attain the notoriety of a Lei Feng, but the Republic of Facebookistan gladly pays them the currency of attention, as long as the investment pays off for top managers and shareholders.

As more people understand the implications of enjoying Facebook "for free"—i.e., that they are the product of the service—they also see that its real paying customers are advertisers. As N. Katherine Hayles has stated, the critical question here is: "will ubiquitous computing be coopted as a stalking horse for predatory capitalism, or can we seize the opportunity" to deploy more emancipatory uses of it? I have expressed faith in the latter possibility, but Facebook continually validates Julie Cohen's critique of a surveillance-innovation complex. The experiment fiasco is just the latest in a long history of ethically troubling decisions at that firm, and several others like it.

Unfortunately, many in Silicon Valley still barely get what the fuss is about. For them, A/B testing is simply a way of life. There are some revealing similarities between casinos and major Internet platforms. As Rob Horning observes, "Social media platforms are engineered to be sticky. . . . Like video slots, which incite extended periods of 'time-on-machine' to assure 'continuous gaming productivity' (i.e. money extraction from players), social-media sites are designed to maximize time-on-site, to make their users more valuable to advertisers . . . and to ratchet up user productivity in the form of data sharing and processing that social-media sites reserve the rights to." That's one reason we get headlines like "Teens Can't Stop Using Facebook Even Though They Hate It." There are sociobiological routes to conditioning action. The platforms are constantly shaping us, based on sophisticated psychological profiles.

Grant Getters and Committee Men

The characteristics of Facebook's model (i.e., exemplary) users in many ways reflect the constraints on the model users in the company—i.e., the data scientists who try to build stylized versions of reality (models) based on certain data points and theories. The Facebook emotion experiment is part of a much larger reshaping of social science. To what extent will academics study data-driven firms like Facebook, and to what extent will they try to join forces with its own researchers to study others?

Present incentives are clear: collaborate with (rather than develop a critical theory of) big data firms. As Zeynep Tufekci puts it, "the most valuable datasets have become corporate and proprietary [and] top journals love publishing from them." "Big data" has an aura of scientific validity simply because of the velocity, volume, and variety of the phenomena it encompasses. Psychologists certainly must have learned *something* from looking at over 600,000 accounts' activity, right?

The problem, though, is that the corporate "science" of manipulation is a far cry from academic science's ethics of openness and reproducibility. That's already led to some embarrassments in the crossover from corporate to academic modeling (such as Google's flu trends failures). Researchers within Facebook worried about multiple experiments being performed at once on individual users, which might compromise the results of any one study. Standardized review could have prevented that. But, true to the Silicon Valley ethic of "move fast and break things," speed was paramount: "There's no review process. Anyone . . . could run a test . . . trying to alter peoples' behavior," said one former Facebook data scientist.

Why are journals so interested in this form of research? Why are academics jumping on board? Fortunately, social science has matured to the point that we now have a robust, insightful literature about the nature of social science itself. I know, this probably sounds awfully meta—exactly the type of navel-gazing Senator Coburn would excommunicate from the church of science. But it actually provides a much-needed historical perspective on how power and money shape knowledge. Consider, for instance, the opening of Joel Isaac's article "Tangled Loops," on Cold War social science:

> During the first two decades of the Cold War, a new kind of academic figure became prominent in American public life: the credentialed social scientist or expert in the sciences of administration who was also, to use the parlance of the time, a "man of affairs." Some were academic high-fliers conscripted into government roles in which their intellectual and organizational talents could be exploited. McGeorge Bundy, Walt Rostow, and Robert McNamara are the archetypes of such persons. An overlapping group of scholars became policymakers and political advisers on issues ranging from social welfare provision to nation-building in emerging postcolonial states. Postwar leaders of the social and administrative sciences such as Talcott Parsons and Herbert Simon were skilled scientific brokers of just this sort: good "committee men," grant-getters, proponents of interdisciplinary inquiry, and institution-builders. This hard-nosed, suit-wearing, business-like persona was connected to new, technologically refined forms of social science.... Antediluvian "social science" was eschewed in favour of mathematical, behavioural, and systems-based approaches to "human relations" such as operations research, behavioral science, game theory, systems theory, and cognitive science.

One of Isaac's major contributions in that piece is to interpret the social science coming out of the academy (and entities like RAND) as a cultural practice: "Insofar as theories involve certain forms of practice, they are caught up in worldly, quotidian matters: performances, comportments, training regimes, and so on." Government leveraged funding to mobilize research to specific ends. To maintain university patronage systems and research centers, leaders had to be on good terms with the grantors. The common goal of strengthening the U.S. economy (and defeating the communist threat) cemented an ideological alliance.

Government still exerts influence in American social and behavioral sciences. But private industry controls critical data sets for the most glamorous, data-driven research. In the Cold War era, "grant getting" may have been the key to economic security, and to securing one's voice in the university. Today, "exit" options are more important than voice, and what better place to exit to than an Internet platform? Thus academic/corporate "flexians"[2] shuttle between the two worlds. Their research cannot be too venal, lest the academy disdain it. But neither can it indulge in, say, critical theory (what would nonprofit social networks look like), just as Cold War social scientists were ill advised to, say, develop Myrdal's or Leontief's theories. There was a lot more money available for the Friedmanite direction economics would, eventually, take.[3]

Intensifying academic precarity also makes the blandishments of corporate data science an "offer one can't refuse." Tenured jobs are growing scarcer. As MOOCmongers aspire to deskill and commoditize the academy, industry's benefits and flexibility grow ever more alluring. Academic IRBs can impose a heavy bureaucratic burden; the corporate world is far more dynamic. (Consider all the defenses of Facebook authored that emphasized how little review corporate research has to go through: satisfy the boss, and you're basically done, no matter how troubling your aims or methods may be in a purely academic context.)

Creating Kinds

So why does all this matter, other than to the quantitatively gifted individuals at the cutting edge of data science? It matters because, in Isaac's words:

> Theories and classifications in the human sciences do not "discover" an independently existing reality; they help, in part, to create it. Much of this comes down to the publicity of knowledge. Insofar as scientific descriptions of people are made available to the public, they may "change how we can think of ourselves, [and] change our sense of self-worth, even how we remember our own past."

It is very hard to develop categories and kinds for Internet firms, because they are so secretive about most of their operations. (And make no mistake about the current PR kerfuffle for Facebook: it will lead the company to become ever more secretive about its data science, just as Target started camouflaging its pregnancy-related ads and not talking to reporters after people appeared creeped out by the uncanny accuracy of its natal predictions.) But the data collection of the firms is creating whole new kinds of people—for marketers, for the NSA, and for anyone with the money or connections to access the information.

More likely than not, encoded in Facebook's database is some new, milder DSM, with categories like the slightly stingy, who need to be induced to buy more; the profligate, who need frugality prompts; the creepy, who need to be hidden in news feeds lest they bum out the cool. Our new "Science Mart" creates these new human kinds, but also alters them, as "new sorting and theorizing induces changes in self-conception and in behavior of the people classified." Perhaps in the future, upon being classified as "slightly depressed" by Facebook, users will see more happy posts. Perhaps the hypomanic will be brought down a bit. Or perhaps if their state is better for business, it will be cultivated and promoted.

You may think that last possibility unfair, or a mischaracterization of the power of Facebook. But shouldn't children have been excluded from its emotion experiment? Shouldn't those whom it suspects may be clinically depressed? Shouldn't some independent reviewer have asked about those possibilities? Journalists try to reassure us that Facebook is better now than it was two years ago. But the power imbalances in social science remain as funding cuts threaten researchers' autonomy. Until research in general is properly valued, we can expect more psychologists, anthropologists, and data scientists to attune themselves to corporate research agendas, rather than questioning why data about users is so much more available than data about company practices.

NOTES

1. Violet Blue, "Facebook: Unethical, untrustworthy, and now downright harmful," *ZDNet*, July 1, 2014, http://www.zdnet.com/facebook -unethical-untrustworthy-and-now-downright-harmful-70000 31106/?s_cid=e539&ttag=e539&ftag=TRE17cfd61.
2. Lisa Margonelli, "Meet the Flexians," *Pacific Standard*, September 9, 2013, http://www.psmag.com/navigation/politics-and-law

/meet-flexians-government-business-media-money-power-wall
-street-65029/.

3. Milton Friedman, "The Methodology of Positive Economics," reprinted from *Essays in Positive Economics* (Chicago: University of
Chicago Press, 1953) at Marxists.org, https://www.marxists.org
/reference/subject/philosophy/works/us/friedman.htm.

THE FUTURE OF HEALTH PRIVACY

Dr. Deborah Peel, MD

B efore we can consider the future of health privacy in the
United States, we must first examine the health technology systems we have today. At issue is the need to safeguard
personal health information. Health information privacy is an
individual's right to control the acquisition, uses, or disclosures
of his or her identifiable health data. Clearly privacy means control over personal data, not secrecy.

The public believes that the Health Insurance Portability
and Accountability Act (HIPAA) protects the privacy of sensitive health data, but the reality is current health information
technology systems prevent patient consent and control over
personal health data. Individuals no longer have control over
the collection and use of personal health information, which
was the case when medical records were kept in paper systems.

CURRENT REALITY

The consequences of current practices are staggering. U.S.
health IT systems are responsible for the greatest ongoing

Dr. Deborah Peel, MD, is the founder of Patient Privacy Rights (PPR), the
world's leading consumer health privacy advocacy organization.

breach of sensitive personal information in the world. Personal health data in the United Sates is bought, sold, and traded by nearly a million health data brokers *millions of times a day, without the knowledge or consent of the individual.* The scale of this systemic privacy breach is larger than Target's data security breach, which affected 40 million credit cards and 70 million phone numbers and e-mail addresses.

Today, health care institutions, government, technology vendors, and health data holders treat patient data like a proprietary asset, as if individuals no longer have fundamental legal or ethical rights to control the use of personal health information.

Details of the hidden use of personal health data are documented in filings for initial public offerings to sell stock at the Securities and Exchange Commission. The business model of leading companies that offer information, services, and technology is buying, selling, and trading personal information. Companies the Government Accountability Office calls "information sellers" and the Federal Trade Commission and 2013 Rockefeller Report call "data brokers" make tens to hundreds of billions of dollars in revenue annually and are not well-known or understood. Quantifying the total annual revenues from the sale and use of sensitive personal health information inside and outside the health care system is very difficult.

The states and federal government sell or disclose personal health data, too. HealthData.gov has released over one thousand data sets of health information for public use, even though the intent of the "open data" movement was to open up data about government, not individuals. All fifty states sell newborn blood spots and thirty-three states sell inpatient and outpatient data.

Further, current health technology systems also make it impossible for individuals to know about the millions of daily human and electronic uses of personal health information in health technology systems. And there is no comprehensive data map that tracks where health data flows.

There is also no accountability or transparency for the collection or use of patient health data. The "accounting for disclosures" of all patient data from electronic health records, as required by the health technology portion of the 2009 American Recovery and Reinvestment Act, has yet to be implemented in regulations. Individuals have no access to "chain of custody" so they can track all users of their most sensitive personal data. Yet personal health information, data about our minds and bodies, is the most valuable commodity of the Digital Age.

HOW DID THIS HAPPEN?

Congress intended to create strong federal data privacy protections for health information inside the health care system. In 2001, the first HIPAA Privacy Rule was implemented by President Bush.

In 2002, it was amended and the right of consent, i.e., to control the use and disclosure of personal health information, was eliminated. "The *consent provisions . . . are replaced* with a new provision . . . that provides regulatory permission for covered entities to use and disclose protected health information for treatment, payment, or health care operations" (emphasis added). This key fact was not reported by the media.

That single sentence changed the HIPAA Privacy Rule into a "data disclosure rule," fueling a vast industry of health data brokers, or "information sellers," that collect, trade, sell, and use personal health data without patients' knowledge or consent. Fair Information Practices and Privacy Enhancing Techniques were not built into current U.S. health IT systems.

The current and previous administrations, Congress, the Department of Health and Human Services, and the health care and health IT industries worked together to open the nation's treasure trove of personal health data for use without patient knowledge or consent. And unfortunately the administration's 2012 Consumer Privacy Bill of Rights excluded personal health data from the broad proposal that individuals should control personal information in electronic systems and online.

There are many good intentions for opening the nation's health data: lowering the costs of health care, improving the quality of health care and population health, improving efficiency, building a learning health care system, enabling research breakthroughs, unleashing innovation, and much more. But like nuclear energy, personal data can be used for good or for harm.

UNINTENDED CONSEQUENCES

The critical problem is that privacy is essential for healing, for quality health care, and for trust. Now personal data about mental health treatment, cancer treatment, sexually transmitted diseases, prescription records, claims data, and personal health information in social media and searches is online and is bought, sold, and traded millions of times a day, inside and outside the health care system.

Right now, every year, 40 to 50 million U.S. patients realize that health technology systems don't have meaningful or comprehensive data privacy protections and act to protect their privacy. Thirty-seven point five million people hide health information every year. And millions more avoid or delay treatment for cancer, mental illness, or sexually transmitted diseases. *They put their health and lives at risk because they know health technology systems don't keep information private.*

Unlike breaches of paper medical records, breaches of electronic health records cannot be fixed and privacy can never be restored. With consumer credit cards, it is possible to close accounts, terminate authorization, and reissue credit cards. Financial risk is quickly minimized. In electronic health care systems, personal health data exists in millions of databases that are unknown and inaccessible to patients. The information can be read by millions of people and machines at the same time. When data breaches occur in the medical field, privacy cannot be restored. There is simply no way to delete sensitive medical information once it is improperly disclosed and distributed across networked information systems.

CONCLUSIONS AND SOLUTIONS

Why should we tolerate technology that causes "bad" data and bad health outcomes for 40 to 50 million people?

A key reason the American Recovery and Reinvestment Act invested $29 billion in health technology systems was to prevent 100,000 medical errors each year. But health data privacy breaches harm 400 to 500 times as many people as are harmed by medical errors. The good intentions of the current and previous administrations could be achieved by using privacy-enhancing technologies and would prevent "bad" data and the resulting bad outcomes that happen now.

Of course privacy should be taken in context. The context is that the public believes personal health data, the most sensitive and revealing information of all, deserves the strongest comprehensive privacy protections of all data and that they should be able to make individual decisions to control its use. Restoring the Hippocratic Oath, which recognized that privacy is essential for healing, also enables trust in health professionals and the health care system. In fact, the need to protect the privacy of personal health data presents the best and strongest "use case" for building strong data privacy protections into electronic systems and online.

To protect personal health data, the United States needs to build and implement privacy-enhancing technologies, such as strong voluntary cyber IDs or credentials, secure e-mail communication systems, tough data access control systems, consent management systems, electronic health records that allow patients to segment (hold back) sensitive information, health databanks, automated downloading of both personal data and lists of all data users, and more. The gaps in law should be replaced with meaningful and comprehensive data privacy protections. Ironclad data privacy and security protections should "follow the data" and apply outside of the health care system, to include all other settings that hold health information, such as school records systems, which often contain students' personal health information.

Ninety-five percent of the U.S. public believes they should be able to make their own decisions about who can see and use personal health data. Steve Jobs's insight that technology can enable individuals to customize their preferences was one of the keys to Apple's success. Innovative health technologies could enable each person to customize exactly which health information they disclose and to whom. Many privacy-enhancing technologies already exist but are not widely used. The lack of "interoperability" of health data today will also be fixed when patients can hold and control the use of their most sensitive electronic asset: personal health data. When patients control personal health data, the greatest problem posed by the use of technology will be solved: the lack of privacy in electronic systems and on the Internet. Sooner or later the public will find out that government and industry eliminated privacy in electronic systems and online.

To restore public trust and willingness to use technology, the future of health privacy will be individual control over health data. Technology products and services will be used to protect individuals' privacy and put them back in control of the collection and use of sensitive health information.

Every other industry now communicates directly and effectively with the public online. We can easily see, control, and transfer money online; we should be able to do the same with personal health information. To succeed and earn our trust, the health care industry and government will have to be as accountable and transparent with health data as banks are with our money in online banking systems. The government and industry should respect and ensure the fundamental right of law-abiding citizens to be "let alone." Like physicians, health technology should heal and do no harm.

ANONYMITY AND FREE SPEECH: CAN ICANN IMPLEMENT ANONYMOUS DOMAIN NAME REGISTRATION?

Stephanie E. Perrin

INTRODUCTION

ICANN, the Internet Corporation for Assigned Names and Numbers, has had a running debate for the past fourteen years about whether or not an individual or an organization must reveal their name, address, and phone number in the WHOIS directory in order to obtain a domain name. That directory is available freely on the Internet and is enforced through the registrars of domain names, who cannot be accredited to sell and issue domain names unless they commit themselves through contract to collect the information from registrants and make it available. The 2013 registration agreement also requires them to escrow, after their last contact with a customer, all kinds of detailed information for eighteen months for law enforcement purposes. The only concession ICANN makes to the reality of data protection law is to permit registrars to apply for a waiver from some of their contractual requirements to collect and disclose data if they can prove that they would be (or have been found to be)

Stephanie E. Perrin spent thirty years in the Canadian federal government, working on information policy and privacy issues.

violating data protection law (because the ICANN is headquartered in California, the law does not prevent this practice). This has made life very difficult for some of the European registrars.[1]

From the beginning civil society has called for privacy protection, not just for individuals, but for small businesses, NGOs, and groups who have a protected right of free speech and assembly. The ability to have an anonymous domain registration would benefit those who exercise their rights of free speech in dangerous territories, or who are fleeing abuse and persecution. This brought about the development of proxy and privacy service providers, who agree to put their information into the directory and obscure the real registrant or licensee. Many registrants provide false information, which has led to calls for greater accuracy, more accountability, and heavier validation responsibilities for the registrars. Law enforcement and intellectual property rights holders want accurate information for investigations and enforcement, and there is now a small economy that relies on WHOIS data to provide value-added services, from market research to trademark monitoring, domain protection, and cybersecurity. The diversity of interests has produced a fairly intractable battle for the past fourteen years, with many WHOIS studies being completed without consensus. It is hoped that the latest report by the Expert Working Group (EWG), which has been eighteen months in the making, will bring some progress.[2]

PROTECTING ENDANGERED INDIVIDUALS AND GROUPS

The recommendation that ICANN should enable a process to provide secure anonymous credentials for endangered individuals and groups to register their domains anonymously is innovative and would be a step forward in protecting free speech. While domain registrations are hardly the most likely way to track down political dissidents or estranged partners, it is a fact that at the moment, many registrars, even proxy registrars, will give up the identity and address of their customers as soon as law enforcement asks. They are also likely to be socially engineered, in cases where registrants fear domestic violence or religious persecution. Having no address and personal details in either the WHOIS registry, the registrar's records, or the required data escrow avoids this risk. It cannot be relied on to protect the identity or whereabouts of the domain name user, but it is an important recognition by ICANN of the right to anonymous speech.

The report provides five examples of different types of registrants who might need secure credentials:

1. *Religious minorities:* Religious groups are persecuted in many countries around the world, and some sects and congregations meet in secret but would like a way to announce to their communities important events, such as weddings, funerals, and times of worship.
2. *Domestic abuse:* Several countries, including Canada and the United States, provide new identities for individuals who are in danger. The most well-known program is the U.S. witness protection program, but there are also provisions for women/men and children fleeing domestic abuse, those fleeing religious sects who have been threatened, and former government operatives of various kinds.

3. *Political speech:* In many countries around the world, those who lose an election can find themselves brought up on charges of treason, fraud, and various other types of malfeasance. There will be many challenges in this category, such as determining who is a recognized blogger at risk, deciding whether environmentalists who advocate breaking existing laws should be protected, etc.

4. *Ethnic or other social groups:* This category includes ethnic groups subject to discrimination, such as the Roma in Europe, minority tribes or immigrant groups in certain countries, and others subject to discrimination. It would include the GLBT community in certain countries, women's rights or education groups, and other diverse types of social activity.

5. *Journalists:* It will be easy to establish credentials for major news organizations such as the *New York Times* and Al Jazeera, but it will be much more difficult for independent journalists, bloggers, and lesser-known publications. It is possible press associations and human rights groups will have suggestions as to how to determine who would be granted a credential. As can be easily imagined, ICANN would be reluctant to open up a field for litigation, so some restrictions would apply or this entire proposal is unlikely to be accepted.

The basic concept is that a person or group who felt they were at risk would apply (most likely through a representative or proxy) to a tribunal or board that ICANN would establish at arm's length. The board would hear representations as to the risk that the person or group would face with accessible data, and most likely would require attesters (depending on the category of requester) to validate the claims. Then the board would authorize the issuing of a secure credential, using any of the secure anonymous credentials on the market, such as Microsoft's U-Prove[3] or IBM's Identity Mixer.[4]

Basically these credentials permit the holder to prove various attributes, such as that he or she has been recognized and authenticated by a trusted authority, or that he or she has paid for a certain right or service. They do not reveal any personal information, but rely on cryptographic proof and digital signatures. Relying parties have secure cryptographic proof that the entity has the authority they are attesting, without needing to know who they are or how they got that authority. This means the vulnerable parties described above, or their representatives, could go to a trusted authority, provide payment for the desired service, and get a trusted credential.

In the domain registration scenario, the recipient of the trusted credential would take it to a privacy/proxy service provider, who would register the domain name and put their own information in the WHOIS database. In the event of domain problems, the real registrant could still be contactable through secure e-mail, and if they did not choose to come forward in the event of disputes, expedited takedown of the domain could be an option.

IMPLEMENTATION CHALLENGES

A number of practical questions arise:

1. *Who decides who is in danger and gets anonymous credentials?* The current suggestion on the table is that

some sort of tribunal should be formed, which would have authority to grant permission.

2. *Who argues for the anonymous registrant?* There is no point in registering anonymously if there are other traces in the system leading back to the registrant. The current proposal is that an agent or recognized group (a press association or council for instance) will have to attest to the validity of the claim, depending on the registrant type.

3. *Who issues the credential, and how is it used?* There are probably many companies who already deal in certificates who would be happy to enter this business. The group or person representing the vulnerable entity would take the board-approved token for a credential to the credential provider, and the provider would issue a secure credential good for an amount of time. This would then be taken to a proxy service provider, whose contact data would appear in the WHOIS registry, and no data about the individual would appear in the ICANN-controlled ecosystem.

4. *How do we know the person is not a fraudster, and how does the system respond if abuse is found?* We have to rely on the attester, and this risk has to remain the responsibility of the groups who attest to the reliability of the credential applicant. When abuse is found, they will have to take responsibility. One bad case of abuse (child abuse, serious trademark infringement, terrorism, etc.) will discredit this system and raise calls for its dissolution.

5. *Who is liable for any abuse?* Secure credentials have a capability to lock identity credentials within and disclose upon abuse. This may have to be utilized in order to allocate liability. It will hardly prove useful in cases of criminal activity, however, and it is likely that expedited takedown of the domain is a better risk mitigation.

When dealing with vulnerable groups, it is important to think of all the potential risks to these stakeholders. While some proxy/privacy services providers will protect their customers against all charges, others will not pick a fight with local law enforcement, powerful business stakeholders, or government actors. This option protects the domain holder from weak service providers, social engineering attempts, hacking, or outright seizure of servers and records. By doing so, it also protects the registrars and the proxy service providers. Neither will know who they are dealing with. This is a difficult concept for some to accept.

IMPLEMENTATION REQUIREMENTS

Civil society at ICANN is already stretched in managing the Internet governance issues currently being discussed, so if this one is to succeed, they will need help from colleagues who do not normally participate at ICANN. What follows is a short list of requirements that need to be addressed in order to assure the chances of success in developing a process that ICANN could implement.

1. A process to establish criteria for eligibility for secure credentials, starting with the example users above and any others that the ICANN community deems appropriate through policy development. This is a detailed policy.
2. Application forms, required attestations, and financial systems, all with a focus on ensuring that the identities of the requesters (and, in some cases, their agents) are protected. In any anonymous system, this is one of the key weak points.
3. An entity such as an independent tribunal or board to evaluate applications for secure credentials and the attestations of trusted parties such as governments who have authorized name changes, United Nations organizations engaged in the protection of refugees, international associations of journalists, etc. This could be a tribunal with representation from the UN, UNESCO, or other bodies. It is likely that it would only be necessary to form a small panel to hear applications.
4. Accredited proxy providers that would be willing to accept secure credentials and the financial systems whereby they would be paid. Currently Bitcoin could be used, but alternative anonymous cash systems should be evaluated.
5. Policies surrounding expedited takedown procedures and other mitigations of abuse need to be developed as part of the overall policy. However, to do this, a detailed risk assessment ought to be performed. It may be that many risks can be well controlled by active monitoring

of the sites. Many dissident sites already need enhanced security because they are constantly targeted for surveillance, so monitoring for abuse would be an inexpensive add-on.

RESIDUAL RISKS

Secure credentials are not in widespread use because, among other reasons, they are complex to implement, particularly with respect to registration and revocation. It has been argued that all parties ought to be eligible for such registration, but given the work threshold required to establish this service and ensure that it is not used for fraudulent or criminal purposes, the EWG considers this approach unfeasible. The EWG recommends that ICANN consider developing secure protected credentials for limited use and ensure entities availing themselves of the service do indeed have legitimate need for this maximum privacy protection.

It is also recognized that once a domain name is registered and the website using that domain name is operational, various kinds of Internet traffic metadata and content may lead to the identification of the domain name user. This is beyond the scope of ICANN's concern, which is solely focused on the domain registration issues and the attendant data that is collected, used, and disclosed to meet defined purposes within ICANN's remit. Information generated from the actual use of a domain name must be the responsibility of the entities obtaining secure protected credentials, and it would be important for civil society groups to provide information underscoring these risks.

SUMMARY OF KEY BENEFITS

To civil society and human rights activists, the arguments for anonymous free speech are well-known and accepted. The evolving Internet ecosystem makes it harder and harder to achieve. As described above, with increasing demands for a responsive, accurate domain name directory, with more discipline in the accreditation and procedures applying to proxy and shield services, it will be important to protect the vulnerable. This system would safeguard those who most need to use the Internet for the purposes of free speech and communication within groups while providing remedies for abuse. It removes a major security risk and potential liability from registrars, who would bear the responsibility for revealing highly sensitive personal information through social engineering attempts. Finally, it would establish procedures for the enablement of vulnerable and disadvantaged groups to benefit from the many advantages of holding their own domains on the Internet.

NOTES

1. M. Neylon, "ICANT Cope with ICANN," *Blacknight Solutions* blog, February 7, 2014, http://blog.blacknight.com/blow-fuse .html (accessed May 28, 2014).
2. It is perhaps worth noting that the author was unfortunately compelled to dissent from the final report because of certain other provisions in it that would negatively impact privacy protections. See www.stephanieperrin.com.
3. http://research.microsoft.com/en-us/projects/u-prove/.
4. http://researcher.watson.ibm.com/researcher/view_project.php ?id=664.

PROTECTING PRIVACY THROUGH COPYRIGHT LAW?

Pamela Samuelson

In making their now-famous argument for recognition of a legal right to privacy, Samuel Warren and Louis Brandeis relied surprisingly heavily on copyright norms and case law to support the idea that privacy was and should be a protectable interest.[1] They observed:

> The common law secures to each individual the right of determining, ordinarily, to what extent his thoughts, sentiments, and emotions shall be communicated to others. Under our system of government, he can never be compelled to express them (except when upon the witness stand); and even if he has chosen to give them expression, he generally retains the power to fix the limits of the publicity which shall be given them. The existence of this right does not depend upon the particular method of expression adopted. It is immaterial whether it be by word or by signs, in painting, by sculpture, or in music. Neither does the existence of the right depend upon the nature or value of the thought or emotions, nor upon the excellence of the means of expression.

Pamela Samuelson is the Richard M. Sherman '74 Distinguished Professor of Law and Information at the University of California at Berkeley and a director of the Berkeley Center for Law & Technology.

> The same protection is accorded to a casual letter or an entry in a diary and to the most valuable poem or essay, to a botch or daub and to a masterpiece. In every such case the individual is entitled to decide whether that which is his shall be given to the public.[2]

The right to control the dissemination of these works may be partly grounded in property rights. But Warren and Brandeis thought that this was not the entire explanation. "[W]here the value of the production is found not in the right to take the profits arising from publication, but in the peace of mind or the relief afforded by the ability to prevent any publication at all, it is difficult to regard the right as one of property, in the common acceptation of that term."[3]

Suppose, for instance, a man recorded in a letter or diary entry that he did not dine with his wife on a certain day. Warren and Brandeis reasoned that "no one into whose hands those papers fall could publish them to the world, even if possession of the documents had been obtained rightfully; and the prohibition would not be confined to the publication of a copy of the letter itself, or of the diary entry; the restraint extends also to a publication of the contents. What is the thing which is protected? Surely, not the intellectual act of recording the fact that the husband did not dine with his wife, but that fact itself. It is not the intellectual product, but the domestic occurrence."[4] The article discussed numerous copyright cases in which copyright claims were used to protect the privacy interests of individuals.[5] Warren and Brandeis concluded that a right to privacy should be recognized as a separate legally protected interest rather than being a nascent interest indirectly protected by copyright or other laws.

One hundred twenty-five years after publication of that seminal article, the right to privacy has become well recognized and much commented upon,[6] even if its scope continues to be the subject of considerable debate and less secure than Warren and Brandeis might have wanted. This essay will consider whether copyright has recently become, at least in some instances, a more effective way to protect privacy interests than privacy law alone would allow.

The limits of privacy law are readily apparent when this right comes into conflict with the right of the press to cover newsworthy events. An illustrative case is *Time, Inc. v. Sand Creek Partners LP.*[7] Time sued Sand Creek to obtain rolls of film taken by one of its photographers of Julia Roberts in her wedding dress on the stage with Lyle Lovett at a concert held at Sand Creek's facility on the day of her marriage to Lovett. Sand Creek officials seized the film from the photographer and refused to return it. Time sued to reclaim possession of the film.

The court recognized that Lovett (and implicitly Roberts) had privacy interests implicated by the photographs and property interests in their likenesses. However, in the court's view, "the 'newsworthiness' of the images depicted on the films has primacy over any privacy rights which Lovett may have in those images. Lovett and Roberts are widely known celebrities and in that sense are public figures and, in addition, their appearance on stage before thousands of people on the day of their highly publicized but theretofore unannounced and private wedding ceremony, with Roberts still wearing her wedding dress, was a newsworthy event of widespread public interest."[8] Time was thus entitled to return of the film and free to publish the photographs in the course of news reporting.

A quartet of recent cases suggests that copyright law may provide, at least in some circumstances, a way to protect privacy interests of individuals depicted in photographs. Factually similar to *Time, Inc. v. Sand Creek* is *Monge v. Maya Magazines, Inc.*[9] Monge was a celebrity singer and model who had kept her marriage to her manager secret from family as well as fans. A celebrity gossip magazine published photographs of the wedding in connection with a news story about the marriage. Monge sued for copyright infringement and a split Ninth Circuit panel ruled in her favor.

The magazine relied on *Nuñez v. Caribbean Int'l News Corp.*[10] in support of its fair use defense. Nuñez owned copyrights in photographs he'd taken for a modeling portfolio of a woman who later became Miss Puerto Rico. *Caribbean News* published some photographs from the portfolio in connection with a controversy about whether the scantily clad person depicted in the photos deserved this crown. The First Circuit in *Nuñez* held that the newspaper had made a transformative use of the photos because it was for a different purpose than the original, namely, to engage in a public debate about her qualifications for this honor. Because Nunez had not taken the photographs with the intent to market them to newspapers, the court saw no harm to the market for his work.

Although the Ninth Circuit recognized that the wedding photographs in *Monge* were newsworthy, it disagreed with Maya's contention that the use was transformative. The court likened Maya's publication of the wedding photos to Reuters's infringing transmission of a video of the Rodney King beating filmed by LA News.[11] The photos were "not physically or creatively transformed" and were unquestionably commercial in nature.[12] Maya supplanted the photographers' right to control first publication of the photographs and right to demand a hefty sum as compensation for the right to publish the photos. Had Maya merely wished to break the news of Monge's wedding, the court noted that Maya could have published information about the marriage certificate. It was not necessary to publish the photos to expose the secret wedding.

In light of cases such as *Time, Inc. v. Sand Creek*, it seems unlikely that Monge could have prevailed on a right-to-privacy claim against the magazine, particularly given that it had done nothing wrongful in obtaining the photographs. Curiously missing from the Ninth Circuit's analysis in *Monge* was any reference to the identity of the author of the wedding photos. Monge herself seems unlikely to have taken the photos, as she and her spouse were the central figures in them. Monge must have purchased the copyrights in order to bring the lawsuit. Most likely the purpose of taking the photographs was to provide the happy couple with memories of this joyous occasion. That purpose, as in *Nuñez*, was substantially different from Maya's purpose in publishing the photos to expose that the singer was indeed married despite her claim of being single. The dissenting judge pointed out that *Monge* sets an unfortunate precedent that public figures might well use to suppress news coverage about their peccadilloes (think of Anthony Weiner's selfie of his private parts).[13]

Balsley v. LFP, Inc.[14] also involved an assertion of copyright claims to protect privacy interests. Balsey was a TV news anchor who participated in a wet T-shirt contest at a bar and danced nude at the event. An amateur photographer took pictures of her in various states of undress and posted the photos online.

An avid reader of *Hustler* magazine found these photos on the Internet and nominated Balsley for *Hustler*'s "hot news babe" contest. *Hustler* published a photograph from the wet T-shirt contest in its magazine. Balsley sued *Hustler* for infringement, having acquired copyright in the photograph in order to suppress further dissemination of the pictures. The Sixth Circuit Court of Appeals ruled in her favor, rejecting *Hustler*'s fair use defense.

Hill v. Public Advocate of the United States[15] is a third such case. It involved a New Jersey homosexual couple who posted online an engagement photograph taken by a college friend named Hill that depicted them holding hands and kissing. Some politically conservative associations in Colorado used the kiss part of the photo in political advertisements targeting state legislators who supported a same-sex marriage bill. Hill sued for copyright infringement and the gay couple sued for misappropriation of their likeness.

The court threw out the misappropriation claim on the ground that the First Amendment protected Public Advocate's use of the likeness because it "reasonably relates to a publication concerning a matter that is newsworthy or of legitimate public concern."[16] However, when it came to the copyright claim, the court saw nothing newsworthy in the use of the kiss part of the photo and little transformative in it either, even though the use was clearly for a different purpose than the original. The photograph was creative and the taking was qualitatively substantial. The court denied Public Advocate's motion for summary judgment on the fair use issue without considering the harm to the market factor.

Garcia v. Google, Inc.[17] is a fourth case of interest. Garcia was an actress hired to play a minor role in a film tentatively titled *Desert Warrior*. She was paid $500 for three and a half days of filming and spoke the lines she was given. Her performance was later spliced into a video entitled *Innocence of Muslims* in which a dubbed-over voice asked if Muhammad was a child molester. After this video was uploaded to YouTube, it became highly controversial in the Muslim world. One Egyptian cleric issued a fatwa against the film and all involved in its making. Garcia received death threats for her role in the video.

Garcia's reaction was to sue Google for copyright infringement, claiming that her performance was an original work of authorship entitled to a separate copyright from that of the film in which it appeared and that she was entitled to an injunction ordering Google to take down the *Innocence of Muslims* video because it infringed the copyright in her performance. In a split decision, the Ninth Circuit ruled in her favor and ordered Google to take down the video. (The order was later modified so that the video minus Garcia's performance could be viewed.)

One can well understand the desires of Monge, Balsley, Hill, the gay couple in *Hill*, and Garcia to challenge unwelcome uses of their images. In each case, there were equities that favored the outcomes these copyright plaintiffs sought that would, in effect, protect privacy and other personal interests they wished to assert. They are not alone in looking to copyright as a tool for protecting privacy interests. Women are looking to copyright to deal with "revenge porn" situations in which they are typically both the authors of sexually explicit photos of themselves and the victims of unwanted posting of the photos online.[18]

One can understand the attraction of copyright claims as a basis for bringing lawsuits because of the strict liability nature of this tort, its generous array of remedies, and the inhospitable reception courts have had to First Amendment defenses in copyright cases. Whether courts should allow copyright claims to protect personal interests in cases such as these is a question left to another day.

Would Warren and Brandeis approve of this renewed direction for copyright law? At first blush, it might seem yes, but upon reflection, this is somewhat in doubt, as these perspicacious authors recognized that copyright's utility in protecting privacy interests was salient only when works were unpublished and that privacy harms were quite different in nature from the market harms with which copyright is mainly concerned.

NOTES

1. Samuel D. Warren and Louis D. Brandeis, "The Right to Privacy," 4 Harv. L. Rev. 193 (1890). More than half of this article discusses copyright norms and case law.
2. Ibid., 198–99.
3. Ibid., 200–201.
4. Ibid., 201.
5. Ibid., 200–214.
6. See, e.g., Neil M. Richards, *The Puzzle of Brandeis, Privacy, and Speech*, 63 Vand. L. Rev. 1295, 1296 (2010) (characterizing the Warren and Brandeis article as a foundational work for the field of privacy law in the United States); Melville B. Nimmer, *The Right of Publicity*, 19 Law & Contemp. Probs. 203 (1954) (characterizing the Warren and Brandeis article as "perhaps the most famous and certainly the most influential law review article ever written").
7. 825 F. Supp. 210 (S.D. Ind. 1993).
8. Ibid., 213.

9. 688 F.3d 1164 (9th Cir. 2012).

10. 235 F.3d 18 (1st Cir. 2000), cited in support of Maya's fair use defense, *Monge*, 688 F.3d at 1172–73.

11. *LA News Serv. v. Reuters Television Int'l*, 149 F.3d 987 (9th Cir. 1998), discussed in *Monge*, 688 F.3d at 1173.

12. *Monge*, 688 F.3d at 1174.

13. Ibid., 1187.

14. 691 F.3d 747 (6th Cir. 2012).

15. 2014 WL 1293524 (D. Colo. 2014).

16. Ibid., *6.

17. 743 F.3d 1258 (9th Cir. 2014).

18. See, e.g., Amanda M. Levendowski, *Using Copyright to Combat Revenge Porn*, NYU J. Intell. Prop. & Ent. L. (2014).

FEAR AND CONVENIENCE

Bruce Schneier

Assaults on privacy are all around us. Governments, corporations, criminals, all of us individually—we're all after each other's data. We're increasingly living our lives under the gaze of others, even if we don't realize it, and often those others are much more powerful than us. Privacy isn't dead, but it's certainly not healthy. And fighting for it can often feel futile.

This is because we're fighting on the wrong playing field. We're debating the technologies while ignoring the psychology. And although privacy definitely is a technology problem, it's even more of a people problem. The greatest challenges to privacy are fear and convenience. While those might seem unrelated, they are linked and reinforce each other. They result in our relinquishing our privacy again and again. And until we get our needs under control, we're not going to have much privacy.

Fear is why we accept privacy invasions from government. It's what led President Bush to authorize draconian surveillance on Americans and non-Americans by the NSA, Congress to retroactively approve many of those programs, and the

Bruce Schneier is an internationally renowned security technologist, called a "security guru" by *The Economist.*

NSA to interpret its authorizations as aggressively as it could. It's why many Americans are okay with NSA eavesdropping, and why President Obama is continuing it. It's why Congress, if forced to subject the NSA to more oversight, will likely end up giving the NSA more invasive authority—they don't want to be the ones to be blamed if they get it wrong.

There are other fears as well. Drug dealing, money laundering, kidnapping, and child pornography are the traditional fears that the FBI uses to justify ever more invasive surveillance, and are why many of us are willing to accept ever less privacy from the government. To someone who is scared, privacy is a luxury item that can be dispensed with.

Convenience is why we allow corporations to invade our privacy. We give companies our data because the results improve our quality of life. We like all the Web apps we use daily. We like letting Flickr store our photos, Google store our e-mail, and Amazon store our e-books and movies. Credit cards are more convenient than cash. Computerized medical records are more convenient than pushing paper. The Nest thermostat is more convenient than its unconnected predecessor and may save you money. And Internet search has totally changed the way people look for information.

The result of all this convenience is a level of surveillance that would have been inconceivable decades ago. We inform our cell phone company of our exact location twenty-four hours a day because we want to receive calls and texts. We alert social networking sites whenever we make a new friend because we want to stay in touch with them. We allow Google to monitor pretty much everything we read because reading it on the Internet is more convenient. And we let other corporations keep copies of all our conversations, because we find it easier to have them on systems that naturally make copies: e-mail, IM, private message, and so on.

Surveillance is the business model of the Internet. Corporations build systems that spy on us, and we allow that in exchange for services. It's why so many things are "free"; companies both use and sell that information for psychological manipulation: advertising.

These two forces work together. There's a public/private surveillance partnership going on. Governments and corporations have largely the same goals, and they help each other. Most government surveillance piggybacks on existing corporate capabilities. And corporations rely on government to keep their surveillance—and the buying and selling of individual surveillance data—legal and largely unregulated. They use each other's laws to protect their own data collection and get around rules that limit their actions. Both are so punch-drunk on our data that there's no real power arguing for meaningful privacy.

We're living in the Golden Age of Surveillance. Technology has advanced to the point where ubiquitous surveillance is not only possible but cheap and easy. Ephemeral conversation is becoming increasingly rare, and will all but disappear when the Internet of Things starts collecting data about our offline activities and lifeloggers like Google Glass start recording everything we see and say. And it will all be stored and analyzed, bought and sold, and used by both governments and corporations to judge, categorize, and manipulate us. All because we're scared of terrorists and we like the convenience of data-based services.

It doesn't have to be this way. Security doesn't require us to give up our privacy. Convenience doesn't, either. We can have the security that comes from allowing governments to use our data to investigate crimes and conspiracies, but we can ensure that they meet legal requirements before they're allowed access to it. We can have the convenience that comes from giving corporations access to our data, but we can regulate how these companies store our data and what else they can do with it. In short, we need to recognize that fear and convenience don't need to result in carte blanche data access and that there are other human values that need to be balanced.

Fear trumps privacy because fear happens in a more primal part of our brain. And convenience trumps privacy because convenience is real and immediate, while the harms from lack of privacy are more abstract and long-term. The problem is that, without reasoned debate, the trajectory of technology is resulting in a level of surveillance that will change society in ways we can just begin to imagine. We need to think about these issues now and decide what sort of society we want to live in, rather than letting these changes just happen to us without consideration.

ENVISIONING PRIVACY IN THE WORLD OF BIG DATA

Christopher Wolf

Big data may be one of the biggest public policy challenges of our time.[1] The debate surrounding big data asks policy makers to weigh compelling interests such as national security, public health and safety, business innovation, and personal benefits against risks to personal privacy and autonomy from high-tech profiling and discrimination, increasingly automated decision making, inaccuracies and opacity in data analysis, and strains in traditional legal protections.[2]

THE ROLE OF FAIR INFORMATION PRACTICES

There is considerable dispute today over how best to properly calibrate Fair Information Practices (FIPs) to protect privacy in the era of big data. Some suggest that foundational privacy practices such as notice and choice and purpose limitation are either impractical or less relevant due to big data and other emerging technologies.[3] While privacy advocates and regulators

Christopher Wolf is director of the Privacy and Information Management Practice at Hogan Lovells US LLP and founder/cochair of the Future of Privacy Forum think tank.

recognize limitations with our notice-and-choice framework, they worry that big data may provide an excuse to override individual rights to facilitate intrusive marketing or ubiquitous surveillance. There still is a role for notice and choice, just as there is need for practical application of the FIPs that account for modern-day technical realities around collection and use of personal data.

Notice often is considered the most "fundamental" principle of privacy protection.[4] At the same time, there is wide acknowledgment that a privacy framework based on notice and choice has significant limitations.[5] The vast majority of consumers do not read privacy policies,[6] which often are complex and lengthy. In the age of big data, the traditional implementation of notice and choice through detailed privacy policies may result in even more unread policies.

Notice and choice presents particular problems for connected devices or other "smart" technologies that will not be equipped with interactive screens or other easily accessible user interfaces. Information collected in "public" spaces and used for data analytics may also prove problematic. Even if technological solutions may help to facilitate notice and choice options, it will be impractical to premise data collection and use in the world of big data and other emerging technologies based solely on traditional implementations of notice and choice.

PRIVACY POLICIES IN THE ERA OF BIG DATA

Privacy policies still have value. They remain accountability and enforcement mechanisms: they set the boundaries for data use by businesses beyond those that might be prescribed by law and they create enforceable legal obligations under consumer protection statutes. Disclosure requirements by themselves can force companies to evaluate their privacy practices and instill discipline in how they treat consumer information.[7]

Most privacy regimes endorse a principle of use limitation, which is generally implemented by requiring that personal information be used *only* as specified at the time of collection.[8] Most of the innovative secondary uses of information—including breakthroughs in medicine, data security, and energy usage—are impossible to anticipate when notice is first provided to individuals, often long before a new benefit is uncovered through data analysis.[9] Companies cannot provide notice for a purpose that is yet to exist, nor can consumers provide informed consent for an unknown use of their data.[10]

However, these principles may be implemented instead by limiting the use of information based upon the *context* in which it is collected.[11] Often, context is understood to mean that personal information should be used only in ways that individuals would expect given the context in which information was disclosed and collected. However, there are uses of data that may be outside individual expectations but have high societal value and minimal privacy impact that should be encouraged. More work is needed to define and frame context.

DATA MINIMIZATION

Overshadowed by the principles of notice and choice,[12] data minimization is another important traditional privacy practice.[13] Data minimization promotes privacy by limiting the amount of personal information in circulation.[14] Yet it is not clear that minimizing information collection is always a practical approach to privacy in the age of big data.[15] Almost by definition, "big" data requires a significant amount of data to be available to discern previously unnoticed patterns and trends. According to a White House report, "wide-ranging data collection may be essential for some familiar and socially beneficial internet services and applications."[16] These uses, as well as many others yet to be developed, would be stymied if organizations were required to limit the amount of data they collect.

ACCOUNTABILITY MECHANISMS

There is still a role for sensible retention policies and limits on data retention. However, concerns around data collection and use may be mitigated through additional accountability measures, such as internal controls and internal review boards. Further, when organizations use adequately de-identified data sets, privacy risks associated with the use of that data can be mitigated, which demonstrates how further research around de-identification could prove helpful within the context of big data. Thus, a more sophisticated analysis of data minimization should take into account the de-identification and other privacy safeguards that have been implemented.

DEFINING PII

Clarifying the scope of information subject to privacy law has become an increasingly important policy question. Personally identifiable information (PII) is one of the central concepts in information privacy regulation, but there is no uniform definition of PII.[17] Similarly, there is no standard for what constitutes adequate de-identification of PII.[18]

This is important because resolving the spectrum of PII and non-PII also addresses some of the concerns facing traditional FIPs. As the Federal Trade Commission acknowledged in its March 2012 report *Protecting Consumer Privacy in an Era of Rapid Change*, data that has been effectively de-identified does not raise significant privacy concerns.[19] However, laws often turn on whether or not information is PII or not, and this bipolar approach based on labeling information either "personally identifiable" or not is not appropriate given the messiness of big data.[20]

De-identification should be understood as a process that takes into account legal and administrative safeguards, as well as technical measures, to protect privacy. Unfortunately, at the moment, much of the discourse around de-identification focuses on the technical possibility of re-identification and the assumption that all data will be made publicly available.[21] While computer scientists have repeatedly shown that anonymized data, either released publicly or poorly de-identified, can be re-identified, organizations and policy makers must recognize that nonpublic data presents a lessened privacy risk compared to information released publicly.

Effective de-identification should consider the legal and administrative controls around data and there remains work to be done to advance technical de-identification measures.

CONTEXT

A principle of respect for context relies on what individuals expect from their relationship with an organization. Consumers expect that companies will share their personal information with other companies to fulfill orders and that companies will use personal information to engage in first-party marketing.[22] When personal information is used in those ways or in others that individuals would reasonably expect, there is no privacy violation.

Respect for context can become difficult to meet when faced with innovative data practices.[23] Focusing solely on individual expectations not only hampers some benefits that could accrue to those individuals, but it also ignores that company-to-consumer relationships evolve. Respect for context must admit that a relationship between an organization and an individual may change over time in ways not foreseeable at the time of collection, and that "such adaptive uses of personal data may be the source of innovations that benefit consumers."[24]

The challenge facing organizations and policy makers is that respect for context requires an appreciation for dynamic social and cultural norms.[25] Context includes not only an objective component, but also a number of subjective variables including an individual's level of trust and his perceived value from the use of his information.[26] Public-facing efforts to inform consumers about big data will be essential to provide individuals with more context around data practices. Companies could frame relationships by "setting the tone" for new products or novel uses of information. Even where new uses of data are contextually similar to existing uses, information and education are essential.

TRANSPARENCY

To complement a principle focused on respect for context, organizations must be much more transparent about how they are using data. Many of the concerns around big data applications center on worries about untoward data usage, and enhanced transparency may help alleviate fears that an individual's personal information is somehow being used against them. Transparency can be a tool that can help demystify big data.[27] For example, organizations should disclose the criteria underlying their decision-making processes to the extent possible without compromising their trade secrets or intellectual property rights. While there are practical difficulties in requiring these disclosures, distinctions can be drawn between sensitive, proprietary algorithms and high-level decisional criteria.

BIG DATA STEWARDSHIP

Big data may warrant a shift in focus toward accountability mechanisms that ensure organizations are responsibly managing personal information.[28] Several privacy scholars have suggested that our current privacy framework stresses mere compliance, when emphasizing institutional accountability may be more necessary to promote better data stewardship.[29] While there are many strategies to augment accountability in the age of big data, it will be important for organizations to engage in a practical balancing of privacy considerations and data use.

A formalized review mechanism could help to review and approve innovative data projects.[30] Some have also called for big data "algorithmists" that could evaluate the selection of data sources, the choice of analytical tools, and the interpretation of any predictive results.[31] As organizations increasingly face interesting new proposals for using data, these professionals could operate across the public and private sectors and conduct cost-benefit analyses of data uses.

Industry increasingly faces ethical considerations over how to minimize data risks while maximizing benefits to all parties. Formal review processes may serve as an effective tool to infuse ethical considerations into data analysis. Institutional review boards (IRBs) were the chief regulatory response to decades of questionable ethical decisions in the field of human subject testing; big data internal review boards could similarly serve as a proactive response to concerns regarding data misuse. In many respects, these review boards would be a further expansion of the role of privacy professionals within the industry today. While creating internal review boards would present a unique set of challenges, encouraging companies to create sophisticated structures and personnel to grapple with these issues and provide oversight would be invaluable.

Any successful approach to big data must be guided by a cost-benefit analysis that takes into account exactly how the benefits of big data will be distributed. So far, our procedural frameworks are largely focused on traditional privacy risks and assessing what measures can be taken to mitigate those risks. In 2010, for example, the Department of Commerce's Internet Policy Task Force endorsed the use of privacy impact assessments (PIAs) both to help organizations decide whether it is appropriate to engage in innovative data uses and to identify alternative approaches that could reduce relevant privacy risks.[32] However, human research IRBs also take into account anticipated benefits and even the importance of any knowledge that may result from research.[33]

CONCLUSION

The White House report on big data well summarized the challenge facing the privacy and technology communities in addressing privacy in a world of technological advances.

> Privacy is an important human value. The advance of technology both threatens personal privacy and provides opportunities to enhance its protection. The challenge for the U.S. Government and the larger community, both within this country and globally, is to understand what the nature of privacy is in the modern world and to find those technological, educational, and policy avenues that will preserve and protect it.[34]

The prospects are good that thoughtful and concerned people will develop needed solutions with greater attention being paid to preserving privacy in our modern society.

NOTES

1. Jules Polonetsky, Omer Tene, and Christopher Wolf, "How to Solve the President's Big Data Challenge," IAPP Privacy Perspectives, January 31, 2014, https://www.privacyassociation.org/privacy_per spectives/post/how_to_solve_the_presidents_big_data_challenge.

2. Leadership Conference, "Civil Rights Principles for the Era of Big Data," press release, http://www.civilrights.org/press/2014/civil -rights-principles-big-data.html (accessed March 15, 2013).

3. The growing network of smart, connected devices known as the

"Internet of Things" commonly is understood to rely upon the capture, sharing, and use of data, including data about who we are and what we do at any given moment. See, e.g., Bill Wasik, "In the Programmable World, All Our Objects Will Act as One," *Wired*, May 14, 2013, http://www.wired.com/gadgetlab/2013/05/internet -of-things/. Providing notice and choice at each instance of collection would be impractical.

4. Federal Trade Commission, *Privacy Online: A Report to Congress*, June 1998, 7, http://www.ftc.gov/sites/default/files/documents/re ports/privacy-online-report-congress/priv-23a.pdf.

5. Fred Cate, "Consumer Protection: Looking Beyond Notice and Choice," *Privacy and Security Law Report*, March 29, 2010, http:// www.hunton.com/files/Publication/f69663d7-4348-4dac-b448 -3b6c4687345e/Presentation/PublicationAttachment/dfdad6 15-e631-49c6-9499-ead6c2ada0c5/Looking_Beyond_Notice_and _Choice_3.10.pdf (citing former FTC chairman Jon Leibowitz conceding that the notice and choice regime offered by the FIPs has not "worked quite as well as we would like").

6. Aleecia M. McDonald and Lorrie Faith Cranor, "The Cost of Reading Privacy Policies," *I/S: A Journal of Law and Policy for the Information Society* 4 (2008): 543.

7. See Peter P. Swire, "The Surprising Virtues of the New Financial Privacy Law," 86 Minn. L. Rev. 1263, 1314 (2002).

8. See, e.g., European Parliament and Council Directive 95/46/EC on the Protection of Individuals with Regard to the Processing of Personal Data and on the Free Movement of Such Data, *Official Journal of the European Union* L 281 (1995): 31, http://www.refworld .org/docid/3ddcc1c74.html (accessed March 15, 2014).

9. Viktor Mayer-Schönberger and Kenneth Cukier, *Big Data* (First Mariner Books, 2014), 153.

10. Ibid.

11. Christopher Wolf and Jules Polonetsky, "An Updated Privacy

Paradigm for the 'Internet of Things,'" Future of Privacy Forum, November 19, 2013, 9, http://www.futureofprivacy.org/wp-content /uploads/Wolf-and-Polonetsky-An-Updated-Privacy-Paradigm -for-the-%E2%80%9CInternet-of-Things%E2%80%9D-11-19 -2013.pdf..

12. Fred H. Cate, The Failure of Fair Information Practice Principles. Consumer Protection in the Age of the Information Economy, 2006, 357–60, http://www.ftc.gov/sites/default/files/documents/public _comments/privacy-roundtables-comment-project-no.p095416 -544506-00057/54450 6-00057.pdf.

13. See Organisation for Economic Co-operation and Development, OECD Guidelines on the Protection of Privacy and Transborder Flows of Personal Data, September 23, 1980, http://www.oecd .org/document/18/0,3343,en_2649_34255_1815186_1_1_1_1,00 .html. Data minimization involves limiting an organization's collection of personal data to the minimum extent necessary to obtain specified and legitimate goals. The principle further instructs organizations to delete data that is no longer used for the purposes for which it was originally collected, and to implement restrictive policies with respect to the retention of personal data in identifiable form.

14. With less data to process and analyze, many believe that companies will have less capability to use data in new, privacy-invasive ways—and consumers will be protected from unwarranted access to their information. See, e.g., Justin Brookman and G.S. Hans, "Why Collection Matters," Future of Privacy Forum, 2013, http:// www.futureofprivacy.org/wp-content/uploads/Brookman-Why -Collection-Matters.pdf.

15. Omer Tene and Jules Polonetsky, "Privacy in the Age of Big Data: A Time for Big Decisions," 64 Stan. L. Rev. Online 63 (2012), http:// www.stanfordlawreview.org/online/privacy-paradox/big-data.

16. White House, "Consumer Data Privacy in a Networked World:

A Framework for Protecting Privacy and Promoting Innovation in the Global Digital Economy," 2012, 21, http://www.whitehouse .gov/sites/default/files/privacy-final.pdf (hereinafter White House Blueprint).

17. Paul M. Schwartz and Daniel J. Solove, "The PII Problem: Privacy and a New Concept of Personally Identifiable Information," 86 NYU L. Rev. 1814 (2011).

18. Paul Ohm, "Broken Promises of Privacy: Responding to the Surprising Failure of Anonymization," 57 UCLA L. Rev. 1701 (2010) (arguing that "scientists have demonstrated that they can often 'reidentify' or 'deanonymize' individuals hidden in anonymized data with astonishing ease." But see Daniel Barth-Jones, "Re-Identification Risks and Myths, Superusers and Super Stories," *Concurring Opinions*, September 6, 2012, http://www.concurring opinions.com/archives/2012/09/re-identification-risks-and-myths -superusers-and-super-stories-part-ii-superusers-and-super-sto ries.html (citing Ohm's suggestion that public policy should not "inappropriately conflat[e] the rare and anecdotal accomplishments of notorious hackers with the actions of typical users").

19. Federal Trade Commission, *Protecting Consumer Privacy in an Era of Rapid Change: Recommendations for Businesses and Policymakers*, March 2012, 20–22, http://www.ftc.gov/sites/default/files /documents/reports/federal-trade-commission-report-protecting -consumer-privacy-era-rapid-change-recommendations/120326 privacyreport.pdf (hereinafter FTC Privacy Report).

20. See generally Mayer-Schönberger and Cukier, 32–49 (suggesting the value of big data may require an approach to data analysis that is "comfortable with disorder and uncertainty").

21. Yianni Lagos and Jules Polonetsky, "Public vs. Nonpublic Data: The Benefits of Administrative Control," 66 Stan. L. Rev. Online 103 (2013), http://www.stanfordlawreview.org/online/privacy-and -big-data/public-vs-nonpublic-data.

22. See White House Blueprint, 16–17.

23. Jules Polonetsky and Omer Tene, "It's Not How Much Data You Have, but How You Use It," Future of Privacy Forum, 2012, 5, http://www.futureofprivacy.org/wp-content/uploads/FPF-White-Paper-Its-Not-How-Much-Data-You-Have-But-How-You-Use-It_FINAL1.pdf.

24. White House Blueprint, 16.

25. Carolyn Nguyen, director, Microsoft Technology Policy Group, Contextual Privacy, address at the FTC Internet of Things Workshop (November 19, 2013) (transcript available at http://www.ftc.gov/sites/default/files/documents/public_events/internet-things-privacy-security-connected-world/final_transcript.pdf).

26. Ibid.

27. Tene and Polonetsky, "Privacy in the Age of Big Data," 270–72.

28. See Fred H. Cate and Viktor Mayer-Schönberger, "Data Use and Impact Global Workshop," December 1, 2013, http://cacr.iu.edu/sites/cacr.iu.edu/files/Use_Workshop_Report.pdf.

29. Ibid., 5.

30. Ryan Calo, "Consumer Subject Review Boards: A Thought Experiment," 66 Stan. L. Rev. Online 97 (2013).

31. Mayer-Schönberger and Cukier, 180.

32. U.S. Department of Commerce Internet Policy Task Force, "Commercial Data Privacy and Innovation in the Internet Economy: A Dynamic Policy Framework," 2010, 34–35, http://www.commerce.gov/sites/default/files/documents/2010/december/iptf-privacy-green-paper.pdf.

33. 45 CFR § 46.111.

34. See Executive Office of the President, "Big Data: Seizing Opportunities, Preserving Values," May 2014, 53.

EPILOGUE:
THE MADRID PRIVACY
DECLARATION—"GLOBAL
PRIVACY STANDARDS FOR
A GLOBAL WORLD"

The Madrid Privacy Declaration was drafted on the occasion of the 2009 International Conference of Data Protection and Privacy Commissioners in Madrid. Several hundred privacy experts and NGOs endorsed the statement. The Madrid Privacy Declaration reaffirms international instruments for privacy protection, identifies new challenges, and call for concrete actions. It remains the most enduring articulation of privacy rights in the modern age.

Affirming that privacy is a fundamental human right set out in the Universal Declaration of Human Rights, the International Covenant on Civil and Political Rights, and other human rights instruments and national constitutions;

Reminding the EU member countries of their obligations to enforce the provisions of the 1995 Data Protection Directive and the 2002 Electronic Communications Directive;

Reminding the other OECD member countries of their obligations to uphold the principles set out in the 1980 OECD Privacy Guidelines;

Reminding all countries of their obligations to safeguard the civil rights of their citizens and residents under the provisions of their national constitutions and laws, as well as international human rights law;

Anticipating the entry into force of provisions strengthening the Constitutional rights to privacy and data protection in the European Union;

Noting with alarm the dramatic expansion of secret and unaccountable surveillance, as well as the growing collaboration between governments and vendors of surveillance technology that establish new forms of social control;

Further noting that new strategies to pursue copyright and unlawful content investigations pose substantial threats to communications privacy, intellectual freedom, and due process of law;

Further noting the growing consolidation of Internet-based services, and the fact that some corporations are acquiring vast amounts of personal data without independent oversight;

Warning that privacy law and privacy institutions have failed to take full account of new surveillance practices, including behavioral targeting, databases of DNA and other biometric identifiers, the fusion of data between the public and private sectors, and the particular risks to vulnerable groups, including children, migrants, and minorities;

Warning that the failure to safeguard privacy jeopardizes associated freedoms, including freedom of expression, freedom of assembly, freedom of access to information, non-discrimination, and ultimately the stability of constitutional democracies;

Civil Society takes the occasion of the 31st annual meeting of the International Conference of Privacy and Data Protection Commissioners to:

(1) Reaffirm support for a global framework of Fair Information Practices that places obligations on those who collect and process personal information and

gives rights to those whose personal information is collected;

(2) Reaffirm support for independent data protection authorities that make determinations, in the context of a legal framework, transparently and without commercial advantage or political influence;

(3) Reaffirm support for genuine Privacy Enhancing Techniques that minimize or eliminate the collection of personally identifiable information and for meaningful Privacy Impact Assessments that require compliance with privacy standards;

(4) Urge countries that have not ratified Council of Europe Convention 108 together with the Protocol of 2001 to do so as expeditiously as possible;

(5) Urge countries that have not yet established a comprehensive framework for privacy protection and an independent data protection authority to do so as expeditiously as possible;

(6) Urge those countries that have established legal frameworks for privacy protection to ensure effective implementation and enforcement, and to cooperate at the international and regional level;

(7) Urge countries to ensure that individuals are promptly notified when their personal information is improperly disclosed or used in a manner inconsistent with its collection;

(8) Recommend comprehensive research into the adequacy of techniques that deidentify data to determine whether in practice such methods safeguard privacy and anonymity;

(9) Call for a moratorium on the development or implementation of new systems of mass surveillance, including facial recognition, whole body imaging, biometric identifiers, and embedded RFID tags, subject to a full and transparent evaluation by independent authorities and democratic debate; and

(10) Call for the establishment of a new international framework for privacy protection, with the full participation of civil society, that is based on the rule of law, respect for fundamental human rights, and support for democratic institutions.

BIBLIOGRAPHY

NEW MODELS OF PRIVACY FOR THE UNIVERSITY
Christine L. Borgman et al.

American Association of University Professors. "Academic Freedom." AAUP.org, 2014. Accessed April 29, 2014. http://www.aaup.org/issues/academic-freedom.

University of California, Office of the President. "Privacy and Information Security Initiative, Final Report." UCOP.edu, 2014. Accessed May 8, 2014. http://ucop.edu/privacy-initiative/.

ACCOUNTABILITY UNCHAINED: BULK DATA RETENTION, PREEMPTIVE SURVEILLANCE, AND TRANSATLANTIC DATA PROTECTION
Kristina Irion

Article 29 Data Protection Working Party. Opinion 04/2014 on Surveillance of Electronic Communications for Intelligence and National Security Purposes. Adopted April 10, 2014. http://ec.europa.eu/justice/data-protection/article-29/documentation/opinion-recommendation/files/2014/wp215_en.pdf.

Bigo, D., S. Carrera, N. Hernanz, J. Jeandesboz, J. Parkin, F. Ragazzi, and A. Scherrer. "Mass Surveillance of Personal Data by EU Member States and Its Compatibility with EU Law." Study for the European Parliament. Brussels: European Union, 2013. http://www.europarl.europa.eu/RegData/etudes/etudes/join/2013/493032/IPOL-LIBE_ET%282013%29493032_EN.pdf.

Bowden, C. "The US Surveillance Programmes and Their Impact on EU Citizens' Fundamental Rights." Study for the European Parliament. Brussels: European Union, 2013. http://www.europarl.europa.eu/meetdocs/2009_2014/documents/libe/dv/briefingnote_/briefingnote_en.pdf.

CJEU. *Digital Rights Ireland and Seitlinger and Others*, Joined Cases C-293/12 and C-594/12, judgment of April 8, 2014. http://curia.europa.eu/juris/document/document.jsf;jsessionid=9ea7d0f130d56dfc652183ac46c28f6fe90119463f54.e34KaxiLc3eQc40LaxqMbN4OaNmNe0?text=&docid=150642&pageIndex=0&doclang=EN&mode=req&dir=&occ=first&part=1&cid=284764.

European Court of Human Rights. *Gabriele Weber and Cesar Richard Savaria v. Germany*, no. 54934/00, decision of June 29, 2006. http://hudoc.echr.coe.int/sites/eng/pages/search.aspx?i=001-76586.

———. *Case of Liberty and Others v. the United Kingdom*, no. 58243/00, judgment of July 1, 2008. http://hudoc.echr.coe.int/sites/eng/pages/search.aspx?i=001-87207.

———. *Centrum för rättvisa v. Sweden*, 35252/08, application of July 14, 2008. http://hudoc.echr.coe.int.

———. *Big Brother Watch and others vs. the United Kingdom*,

58170/13, application of September 4, 2013. http://hudoc
.echr.coe.int/sites/eng/pages/search.aspx?i=001-140713.

European Parliament and the Council of the European Union.
Directive 2006/24/EC of the European Parliament and of the
Council of 15 March 2006 on the Retention of Data Gener-
ated or Processed in Connection with the Provision of Pub-
licly Available Electronic Communications Services or of
Public Communications Networks and Amending Direc-
tive 2002/58/EC. OJ L105/54. 2006. http://eur-lex.europa.eu
/LexUriServ/LexUriServ.do?uri=OJ:L:2006:105:0054:0063
:EN:PDF.

European Parliament. European Parliament Resolution of July 4,
2013, on the US National Security Agency Surveillance Programme, Surveillance Bodies in Various Member States and
Their Impact on EU Citizens' Privacy (2013/2682(RSP).
http://www.europarl.europa.eu/sides/getDoc.do?pubRef
=-//EP//TEXT+TA+P7-TA-2013-0322+0+DOC+XML+V0
//EN.

German Federal Constitutional Court. 1 BvR 256/08, judgment
of March 2, 2010, BVerfGE 125, 260. http://www.bverfg.de
/entscheidungen/rs20100302_1bvr025608.html.

Irion, K. "International Communications Tapped for Intelligence-
Gathering." *Communications of the ACM* 52, no. 2 (February
2009): 26–2.

———. "Government Cloud Computing and the National
Data Sovereignty." *Policy and Internet* 4, no. 3 (2012): 40–71.

NETmundial. "NETmundial Multistakeholder Statement." São
Paulo, Brazil, April 24, 2014. http://netmundial.br/netmun
dial-multistakeholder-statement/.

UN General Assembly. "The Right to Privacy in the Digital Age." Resolution adopted on the 68th General Assembly. December 18, 2013. http://daccess-dds-ny.un.org/doc/UN DOC/GEN/N13/449/47/PDF/N1344947.pdf?OpenElement.

UN News Center. "General Assembly Backs Right to Privacy in Digital Age." December 19, 2013. http://www.un.org/ga /search/view_doc.asp?symbol=A/C.3/68/L.45/Rev.1.

U.S. Congress. Foreign Intelligence Surveillance Act of 1978 Amendments Act of 2008, 122 Stat. 2436, Public Law 110–261. July 10, 2008. http://www.gpo.gov/fdsys/pkg/PLAW -110publ261/pdf/PLAW-110publ261.pdf.

U.S. Mission to the EU. "Five Myths Regarding Privacy and Law Enforcement Access to Personal Information in the EU and the US." 2012. http://photos.state.gov/libraries/us eu/231771/PDFs/Five%20Myths%20Regarding%20Priva cy%20and%20Law%20Enforcement_October%209_2012 _pdf.pdf.

"RESPECT FOR CONTEXT": FULFILLING THE PROMISE OF THE WHITE HOUSE REPORT
Helen Nissenbaum

Civil, C. "President Obama's Privacy Bill of Rights: Encouraging a Collaborative Process for Digital Privacy Reform." *Berkeley Technology Law Journal*, March 12, 2012.

Department of Commerce National Telecommunications and Information Administration. "Consumer Data Privacy in a Networked World: A Framework for Protecting Privacy and Promoting Innovation in the Global Digital Economy." White House Privacy Report, February 23, 2012.

Electronic Privacy Information Center. "White House Sets Out Consumer Privacy Bill of Rights." EPIC.org, February 23, 2012.

Hoffman, D. "White House Releases Framework for Protecting Privacy in a Networked World." *Policy@Intel* blog, February 23, 2012.

Hoffman, M. "Obama Administration Unveils Promising Consumer Privacy Plan, but the Devil Will Be in the Details." Electronic Frontier Foundation, February 23, 2012.

Nissenbaum, H. *Privacy in Context: Technology, Policy and the Integrity of Social Life.* Stanford, CA: Stanford Law, 2010.

———. "A Contextual Approach to Privacy Online." *Daedalus* 140, no. 4 (2011): 32–48.

Organisation for Economic Co-operation and Development. "OECD Guidelines on the Protection of Privacy and Transborder Flows of Personal Data." September 23, 1980.

ANONYMITY AND FREE SPEECH: CAN ICANN IMPLEMENT ANONYMOUS DOMAIN NAME REGISTRATION?
Stephanie E. Perrin

Internet Corporation for Assigned Names and Numbers (ICANN). "Final Report from the Expert Working Group on gTLD Directory Services: A Next-Generation Registration Directory Service." 2014. https://www.icann.org/en/system/files/files/final-report-06jun14-en.pdf.

REFERENCES

EPIC REFERENCES

EPIC's work is available on the EPIC website, www.epic.org. A summary of the key categories follows.

EPIC Alert
  epic.org/alert/

EPIC Publications
  epic.org/bookstore/epic_books.html

EPIC in the News
  epic.org/news/epic_in_news.html

EPIC Events
  epic.org/events

EPIC Advisory Board
  epic.org/about/advisory-board/

EPIC Open Government Project
  epic.org/foia

EPIC Amicus Briefs
  epic.org/amicus

EPIC Consumer Protection Project
  epic.org/privacy/consumer

EPIC Administrative Law Project
epic.org/apa/comments

CONTRIBUTOR WORKS

Steven Aftergood
http://fas.org/expert/steven-aftergood/

Ross Anderson
http://www.cl.cam.ac.uk/~rja14/

Christine L. Borgman
http://christineborgman.info/

Ryan Calo
http://www.law.washington.edu/directory/Profile.aspx
?ID=713

Danielle Citron
http://www.law.umaryland.edu/faculty/profiles/faculty
.html?facultynum=028

Simon Davies
http://www.privacysurgeon.org/blog/about/

A. Michael Froomkin
http://www.law.miami.edu/faculty-administration/michael
-froomkin.php?op=1

Kristina Irion
http://people.ceu.hu/kristina_irion

Jeff Jonas
http://jeffjonas.typepad.com/

Harry Lewis
http://lewis.seas.harvard.edu/

Anna Lysyanskaya
    http://cs.brown.edu/people/anna/

Gary T. Marx
    http://web.mit.edu/gtmarx/www/garyhome.html

Aleecia M. McDonald
    http://cyberlaw.stanford.edu/about/people/aleecia-mcdonald

Dr. Pablo G. Molina
    http://www.educause.edu/members/pablo-garcia-molina

Peter G. Neumann
    http://www.csl.sri.com/users/neumann/

Helen Nissenbaum
    http://www.nyu.edu/projects/nissenbaum/

Frank Pasquale
    http://law.shu.edu/Faculty/fulltime_faculty/Frank-Pasquale
    .cfm

Dr. Deborah Peel, MD
    http://patientprivacyrights.org/board-of-directors
    /#deborah

Stephanie E. Perrin
    http://idtrail.org/content/view/51/43/

Pamela Samuelson
    https://www.law.berkeley.edu/phpprograms/faculty/faculty
    Profile.php?facID=346

Bruce Schneier
    https://www.schneier.com

Christopher Wolf
    http://www.hoganlovells.com/christopher-wolf/

BIOGRAPHIES

Steven Aftergood

Steven Aftergood is a senior research analyst at the Federation of American Scientists. He directs the FAS Project on Government Secrecy, which works to reduce the scope of government secrecy and to promote public access to government information. His blog *Secrecy News* reports on current developments in secrecy policy and provides direct public access to valuable government records that are otherwise hard to find. In 1997, Mr. Aftergood was the plaintiff in a Freedom of Information Act lawsuit against the Central Intelligence Agency that led to the declassification and publication of the total intelligence budget ($26.6 billion in 1997) for the first time in fifty years. In 2006, he won a FOIA lawsuit against the National Reconnaissance Office for release of unclassified budget records. Mr. Aftergood is an electrical engineer by training.

Ross Anderson

Ross Anderson is professor of security engineering at the Computer Laboratory, University of Cambridge, and a fellow of the Royal Society, the Royal Academy of Engineering, the Institution of Engineering and Technology, the Institute of Mathematics and Its Applications, and the Institute of Physics. He also chairs the Foundation for Information Policy Research, the UK's leading Internet policy think tank, which he helped set up in 1998.

Christine L. Borgman

Christine L. Borgman, professor and presidential chair in information studies at UCLA, is the author of more than two hundred publications in information studies, computer science, and communication. Her monographs *Scholarship in the Digital Age: Information, Infrastructure, and the Internet* (MIT Press, 2007) and *From Gutenberg to the Global Information Infrastructure: Access to Information in a Networked World* (MIT Press, 2000) each won the Best Information Science Book of the Year award from the American Society for Information Science and Technology. Her book, *Big Data, Little Data, No Data: Scholarship in the Networked World*, was published by MIT Press in January 2015. She is a fellow of the American Association for the Advancement of Science and of the Association for Computing Machinery. She is a member of the board of directors of the Electronic Privacy Information Center and previously served on the U.S. National Academies' Board on Research Data and Information and the U.S. National CODATA.

Ryan Calo

Ryan Calo is an assistant professor at the University of Washington School of Law and an affiliate scholar at the Stanford Center for Internet and Society. Professor Calo researches the intersection of law and emerging technology, with an emphasis on robotics and the Internet. His work on drones, driverless cars, privacy, and other topics has appeared in law reviews and major news outlets, including the *New York Times*, the *Wall Street Journal*, and NPR. Professor Calo has also testified before the full Judiciary Committee of the U.S. Senate.

Danielle Citron

Danielle Citron is the Lois K. Macht Research Professor and Professor of Law at the University of Maryland School of Law. Her book, *Hate Crimes in Cyberspace*, was published by Harvard University Press in September 2014.

Simon Davies

Simon Davies founded Privacy International in 1990 and served as director general until 2012, when he left to pursue other projects. Over his twenty-five-year career in privacy he has led campaigns and research initiatives around the world. Until recently he was a visiting senior fellow at the London School of Economics and Political Science, and a fellow of the Chartered Institute for IT (FBCS). He is also co-director of the LSE's Policy Engagement Network. In April 1999 Davies received the Electronic Frontier Foundation's Pioneer Award for his contribution to online freedom, and in 2007 he was made a fellow of the British Computer Society. In both 2004 and 2005 Silicon .com voted him one of the world's fifty most influential people in technology policy. He now writes the *Privacy Surgeon* blog.

A. Michael Froomkin

A. Michael Froomkin is the Laurie Silvers and Mitchell Rubenstein Distinguished Professor of Law at the University of Miami in Coral Gables, Florida, specializing in Internet law and administrative law. He is the founder and editor of the online law review *Jotwell: The Journal of Things We Like (Lots)*, and the founder of the annual We Robot conference on robotics law and policy. He serves on the editorial boards of *Information, Communication and Society* and of *I/S: A Journal of Law and Policy for the Information Society*. Professor Froomkin is on the advisory boards of several organizations, including the Electronic Frontier Foundation and the Electronic Privacy Information Center. Professor Froomkin is a member of the Royal Institute of International Affairs in London, and a nonresident Fellow of the Center for Democracy and Technology and the Yale Law School Information Society Project. Before entering teaching, Professor Froomkin practiced international arbitration law in the London office of Wilmer, Cutler & Pickering. He clerked for Judge Stephen F. Williams of the U.S. Court of Appeals, DC Circuit, and Chief Judge John F. Grady of the U.S. District Court, Northern District of Illinois. Professor Froomkin received his JD from Yale Law School, where he served as articles editor of both the *Yale Law Journal* and the *Yale Journal of International Law*. He has an M.Phil in history of international relations from Cambridge University in England, which he obtained while on a Mellon fellowship. His BA from Yale was in economics and history, summa cum laude, Phi Beta Kappa with distinction in history.

Julia Horwitz

Julia Horwitz is the consumer protection counsel and open government coordinator at EPIC. Her work focuses on consumer privacy and the role of the Federal Trade Commission in protecting consumer data. Ms. Horwitz has also served as adjunct professor of law at the Georgetown University Law Center, where she taught a class on litigating the federal open government laws. She is the coauthor of an article in the *Indiana Law Review* on the pedagogy of teaching open government as a clinical course. Prior to joining EPIC, Ms. Horwitz graduated from the University of Chicago Law School, where she was the vice president for media and technology of the Intellectual Property Law Society. Her BA from Brown University was in American literature, magna cum laude, Phi Beta Kappa, with honors.

Deborah Hurley

Deborah Hurley is the principal of the consulting firm she founded in 1996, which advises governments, international organizations, nongovernmental organizations, and foundations on advanced science and technology policy. She is a fellow of the Institute for Quantitative Social Science at Harvard University. At the Organisation for Economic Co-operation and Development, in Paris, France, she identified emerging legal, economic, social, and technological issues related to information and communications technologies, biotechnology, environmental and energy technologies, nanotechnology, technology policy, and other advanced technology fields. She was responsible for drafting, negotiation, and adoption of the OECD Guidelines for the Security of Information Systems. She directed the Harvard University Information Infrastructure Project. Hurley is the former chair of the board of directors of the Electronic Privacy Information Center and has served on many other governmental and nongovernmental boards and committees, including for the U.S. State Department, the American Association for the Advancement of Science, and the National Academy of Sciences Research Council. She carried out a Fulbright study of intellectual property protection and technology transfer in Korea. She is the author of *Pole Star: Human Rights in the Information Society*, "Information Policy and Governance" in *Governance in a Globalizing World*, and other publications. Hurley received the Namur Award of the International Federation of Information Processing in recognition of outstanding contributions, with international impact, to awareness of social implications of information technology.

Kristina Irion

Kristina Irion is assistant professor at the Department of Public Policy and research director of public policy with the Center for Media and Communications Studies at Central European University (CEU). She is a qualified lawyer; earned her PhD degree from Martin Luther University, Halle-Wittenberg, Germany; and holds a master's degree in information technology and telecommunications law from the University of Strathclyde, Glasgow, UK. Before joining CEU in 2007, she was a part-time counsel with the Berlin Office for Data Protection and Freedom of Information and worked as senior regulatory counsel for a German mobile phone network operator. Irion also gained working experience as a trainee at the European Commission in Brussels and was a visiting fellow at the Electronic Privacy Information Center in Washington.

Jeff Jonas

Jeff Jonas is an IBM fellow and chief scientist of context computing. Jonas's work in context-aware computing was originally developed at Systems Research and Development (SRD), founded by Jonas in 1985 and acquired by IBM in January 2005.

Prior to SRD's acquisition, Jonas spearheaded the design and development of a number of innovative systems, including technology used by the Las Vegas gaming industry. One such innovation played a pivotal role in protecting that industry from aggressive card-count teams. The most notable, known as the "MIT team," was featured in the book *Bringing Down the House* and the movie *21*. This work has also been featured in documentaries aired on the Discovery Channel, the Learning Channel, and the Travel Channel, among others. Today, Jonas is working on a new generation of context computing code-named "G2."

Harry Lewis

Harry R. Lewis is Gordon McKay Professor of Computer Science at Harvard University, where he has taught since 1974 and is a faculty fellow of the Berkman Center for Internet and Society. Among his books are *Blown to Bits: Your Life, Liberty, and Happiness After the Digital Explosion* (with Hal Abelson and Ken Ledeen, Prentice Hall, 2008) and *Excellence Without a Soul: Does Liberal Education Have a Future?* (PublicAffairs, 2007). From 1995 to 2003 Lewis served as dean of Harvard College. He holds an AB, summa cum laude, and PhD in applied mathematics from Harvard.

Anna Lysyanskaya

Anna Lysyanskaya is a professor of computer science at Brown University. She received an AB in computer science and mathematics from Smith College in 1997, and a PhD in computer science and electrical engineering from MIT in 2002. She is a recipient of an NSF CAREER award and a Sloan Foundation fellowship and was included in *Technology Review* magazine's list of thirty-five innovators under thirty-five for 2007. In 2012, she was elected a director of the International Association for Cryptologic Research. Lysyanskaya's research interests are in cryptography, theoretical computer science, and computer security. A theme of her research is balancing privacy with accountability, and specifically allowing users to prove that they are authorized even while not revealing any additional information about themselves. Her work in this area was incorporated into the Trusted Computing Group's industrial standard, served as the theoretical foundation for IBM Zurich's Idemix project, and informed the National Strategy for Trusted Identities in Cyberspace (NSTIC).

Gary T. Marx

Gary T. Marx is professor emeritus at M.I.T. and has also taught at Harvard University, the University of California at Berkeley, and the University of Colorado and schools in Europe and Asia. He has worked in the areas of race and ethnicity, collective behavior and social movements, law and society, and surveillance studies. Among other books he is the author of *Protest and Prejudice, Undercover: Police Surveillance in America, Collective Behavior and Social Movements* (with D. McAdam), *Undercover: Police Surveillance in Comparative Perspective* (with C. Fijnaut), and most recently, *Windows into the Soul: Surveillance and Society in an Age of High Technology*. His work has appeared or been reprinted in over three hundred books, monographs and periodicals and has been widely translated. He has written twelve introductions to colleague's books and published sixteen co-authored works with his students. He has been a research associate at the Harvard-MIT Joint Center for Urban Studies and Harvard Law School Criminal Justice Center, and a fellow at the Stanford Center for Advanced Study in the Behavioral Sciences (1987–88; 1996–97) and the Woodrow Wilson International Center for Scholars (1997–98). He is the recipient of a Guggenheim Fellowship and he has received grants from organizations such as the National Institute of Justice, National Science Foundation, and the Twentieth Century Fund. He has been a consultant to, or served on panels for, national commissions, Senate and House committees, the General Accounting Office, the Office of Technology Assessment, the Justice Department, the National Academy of Sciences, public interest groups, and foundations and think tanks.

Aleecia M. McDonald

Aleecia M. McDonald is the director of privacy at Stanford's Center for Internet and Society. Her research focuses on the public policy issues of Internet privacy and includes user expectations for Do Not Track, behavioral economics and mental models of privacy, and the efficacy of industry self-regulation. She cochaired, and remains active in, the WC3's Tracking Protection Working Group, an ongoing effort to establish international standards for a Do Not Track mechanism that users can enable to request enhanced privacy online. This effort brings together over one hundred international stakeholders from industry, academia, civil society, privacy advocates, and regulators to reach an open, consensus-based multiparty agreement that will establish a baseline for what sites must do when they comply with an incoming request for user privacy. McDonald's decade of experience working in software startups adds a practical focus to her academic work, and she was a senior privacy researcher for Mozilla (part-time, 2011–12) while working for CIS as a resident fellow (part-time, 2011–12.) She holds a PhD in engineering and public policy from Carnegie Mellon, where she studied online privacy as a member of the Cylab Usable Privacy and Security (CUPS) research laboratory. Her findings have been featured in media outlets such as the *Washington Post, Ars Technica,* and Free Press's *Media Minute.* She has presented findings in testimony to the California Assembly and contributed to testimony before the U.S. Senate and the Federal Trade Commission.

Dr. Pablo G. Molina

Dr. Pablo G. Molina is the chief information officer at the American Association of Law Schools and at Southern Connecticut State University. He is also an adjunct professor at Georgetown University, where he teaches graduate courses in ethics and technology management, managing information security, and Internet governance. He is the executive director of the International Applied Ethics and Technology Association. Molina has a doctorate degree from Georgetown University on the adoption of technology in higher education. He is a certified information systems security professional and a certified information privacy professional. He serves on the boards of the Electronic Privacy Information Center and the Hispanic Technology Council. He regularly speaks at conferences on technology, education, and policy, e.g., United Nations and U.S. Internet governance forums, the International Conference of Data Protection and Privacy Commissioners, and information security forums.

Peter G. Neumann

Peter G. Neumann (Neumann@CSL.sri.com) has doctorates from Harvard and Darmstadt. After ten years at Bell Labs in Murray Hill, New Jersey, in the 1960s, he has been at SRI's Computer Science Lab since September 1971 and is now its senior principal scientist. He is currently PI on two DARPA projects: clean-slate trustworthy hosts for the CRASH program with new hardware and new software, and clean-slate networking for the Mission-Oriented Resilient Clouds program. He moderates the ACM Risks Forum (http://www.risks.org), has been responsible for CACM Inside Risks series articles since June 1990, chairs the ACM Committee on Computers and Public Policy, and chaired the National Committee for Voting Integrity as an EPIC project. He is a fellow of the ACM, IEEE, and AAAS, and is also an SRI fellow. Dr. Neumann received the National Computer System Security Award in 2002, the ACM SIGSAC Outstanding Contributions Award in 2005, and the Computing Research Association Distinguished Service Award in 2013. In 2012, he was elected to the newly created National Cybersecurity Hall of Fame as one of the first set of inductees.

Helen Nissenbaum

Helen Nissenbaum is professor of media, culture, and communication, and computer science, at New York University, where she is also director of the Information Law Institute. Her work spans social, ethical, and political dimensions of information technology and digital media. She has written and edited seven books, including *Values at Play in Digital Games* (with Mary Flanagan, MIT Press, 2014) and *Privacy in Context: Technology, Policy, and the Integrity of Social Life* (Stanford University Press,

2010), and her research publications have appeared in journals of philosophy, politics, law, media studies, information studies, and computer science. The National Science Foundation, Air Force Office of Scientific Research, Ford Foundation, U.S. Department of Homeland Security, and U.S. Department of Health and Human Services Office of the National Coordinator have supported her work on privacy, trust online, and security, as well as several studies of values embodied in computer system design, search engines, digital games, facial recognition technology, and health information systems. Nissenbaum holds a PhD in philosophy from Stanford University and a BA (hons.) from the University of the Witwatersrand. Before joining the faculty at NYU, she served as associate director of the Center for Human Values at Princeton University.

Frank Pasquale

Frank Pasquale has taught information and health law at Seton Hall since 2004. He has published over twenty scholarly articles and is currently writing a book called *The Black Box Society: Technologies of Search, Reputation, and Finance* (under contract with Harvard University Press). Pasquale's research agenda focuses on challenges posed to information law by rapidly changing technology, particularly in the health care, Internet, and finance industries. Pasquale has been a visiting fellow at Princeton's Center for Information Technology, and a visiting professor at Yale Law School and Cardozo Law School. He was a Marshall scholar at Oxford University. He has testified before the Judiciary Committee of the House of Representatives, appearing with the general counsels of Google, Microsoft, and Yahoo. He has also presented before a Department of Health and Human Services/Federal Trade Commission roundtable and panels of the National Academy of Sciences. Pasquale is a member of the Harvard-Georgetown Working Group on Market Democracy and an affiliate fellow of Yale Law School's Information Society Project. He has been named to the advisory board of the Electronic Privacy Information Center. He is on the executive board of the health law section of the American Association of Law Schools (AALS) and has served as chair of the AALS section on privacy and defamation.

Dr. Deborah Peel, MD

In 2004, Dr. Deborah Peel founded Patient Privacy Rights (PPR), the world's leading consumer health privacy advocacy organization. PPR has over twelve thousand members from all fifty states. In 2007, she founded the bipartisan Coalition for Patient Privacy, representing 10.5 million U.S. citizens who want to control the use of personal health data in electronic systems. In 2007–2008, she led the development of PPR's Trust Framework, seventy-five-plus auditable criteria that measure how effectively technology systems protect data privacy. The framework can be used for research about privacy and to certify HIT systems. In 2011, Dr. Peel created the International Summits on the Future of Health Privacy, cohosted by Georgetown Law Center. In 2012, her chapter in *Information Privacy in the Evolving Healthcare Environment* laid out a five-year plan to move the U.S. health IT system from institutional to patient control over health data. Dr. Peel was named one of the "100 most influential in healthcare" in the United States by *Modern Healthcare* magazine in 2007, 2008, 2009, and 2011—the first and only privacy expert ever listed.

Stephanie E. Perrin

Stephanie E. Perrin spent thirty years in the Canadian federal government, working on information policy and privacy issues. She was director of privacy policy, responsible for developing private-sector privacy legislation (PIPEDA), leaving in 2000 to work for Zero Knowledge Systems to promote technology for anonymity on the Internet. She is currently a PhD candidate at the University of Toronto Faculty of Information, with research interests focusing on why privacy is not implemented in Internet standards and functions. She is a member of the Expert Working Group at ICANN, tasked with revamping the WHOIS directory, and her research examines why privacy has developed into such an intractable problem at ICANN. This research examines concepts of identity online and the inadequacy of current privacy norms.

Marc Rotenberg

Marc Rotenberg is president and founder of the Electronic Privacy Information Center (EPIC). He teaches privacy law and open government law at Georgetown Law Center. He frequently testifies before Congress and files amicus briefs in federal and state courts on emerging privacy issues. He has published widely in academic journals and served on many expert panels. He is the co-editor of *Technology and Privacy: The New Landscape* (MIT Press, 1998), one of the first anthologies to explore the intersection of law and technology, as well as *Information Privacy Law* (Aspen, 2006) and *Privacy and Human Rights: An International Survey of Privacy Law and Developments* (EPIC, 2006). He is a graduate of Harvard College and Stanford Law School, and received an LLM in international and comparative law from Georgetown.

Pamela Samuelson

Pamela Samuelson is the Richard M. Sherman '74 Distinguished Professor of Law and Information at the University of California at Berkeley and a director of the Berkeley Center for Law and Technology. She has written and spoken extensively about the challenges that new information technologies pose for traditional legal regimes, especially for intellectual property law. She is a member of the American Academy of Arts and Sciences, a fellow of the Association for Computing Machinery (ACM), a contributing editor of *Communications of the ACM*, a past fellow of the John D. and Catherine T. MacArthur Foundation, and an honorary professor of the University of Amsterdam. She is a member of the board of directors of the Electronic Frontier Foundation and of the advisory board of the Electronic Privacy Information Center.

Bruce Schneier

Bruce Schneier is an internationally renowned security technologist, called a "security guru" by *The Economist*. He is the author of twelve books—including *Liars and Outliers: Enabling the Trust Society Needs to Survive*—as well as hundreds of articles, essays, and academic papers. His influential newsletter *Crypto-Gram* and blog *Schneier on Security* are read by more than 250,000 people. Schneier is a fellow at the Berkman Center for Internet and Society at Harvard Law School, a program fellow at the New America Foundation's Open Technology Institute, a board member of the Electronic Frontier Foundation, and an advisory board member of the Electronic Privacy Information Center. He is also the chief technology officer of Co3 Systems Inc.

Jeramie Scott

Jeramie Scott is the national security counsel and privacy co-alition coordinator for EPIC. His work focuses on the privacy issues implicated by drones, biometrics, big data, and license plate readers. He runs the Privacy Coalition, which brings together consumer and privacy organizations with Washington decision makers. Prior to joining EPIC, Mr. Scott graduated from the New York University School of Law, where he was a clinic intern at the Brennan Center's Liberty and National Security Program. Mr. Scott was a member of NYU's Privacy Research Group—a weekly discussion of topical privacy issues and research run by Professor Helen Nissenbaum. Mr. Scott holds a bachelor of science in symbolic systems and a master's degree in philosophy, both from Stanford University.

Christopher Wolf

Christopher Wolf, a member of the EPIC advisory board, is director of the privacy and information management practice at Hogan Lovells US LLP and founder/cochair of the Future of Privacy Forum think tank. He is one of the first practitioners to focus on privacy law, and his practice evolved from an EPIC-referred pro bono case representing a gay service member whose privacy rights were violated by the navy. He created the first privacy law treatise for the Practicing Law Institute and is a frequent author and speaker on privacy law issues. He is a member of the American Law Institute and its Restatement of Privacy project. *Washingtonian* magazine dubbed Wolf a "Tech Titan" and MSNBC called him a "pioneer in Internet law."

INDEX

PUBLISHING IN THE PUBLIC INTEREST